access to history

in depth

The SPANISH CIVIL WAR

Patricia Knight

access to history

in depth

The SPANISH CIVIL WAR

Patricia Knight

Hodder & Stoughton

A MEMBER OF THE HODDER HEADLINE GROUP

Orders: please contact Bookpoint Ltd, 39 Milton Park, Abingdon, Oxon
OX14 4TD. Telephone: (44) 01235 400414, Fax: (44) 01235 400454.
Lines are open from 9.00 - 6.00, Monday to Saturday, with a 24 hour
message answering service. Email address: orders@bookpoint.co.uk

British Library Cataloguing in Publication Data

A catalogue for this title is available from the British Library

ISBN 0 340 70137 4

First published 1998

Impression number	10	9	8	7	6	5	4	3	2
Year			2004	2003	2002	2001	2000		

Cover photo from Weidenfeld and Nicolson Archives

Illustrations by Ian Foulis & Associates Ltd, Saltash
Typeset by Sempringham publishing services, Bedford
Printed in Great Britain for Hodder & Stoughton Educational,
a division of Hodder Headline Plc, 338 Euston Road, London NW1 3BH
by Redwood Books, Trowbridge, Wiltshire.

Contents

Preface

The original *Access to History* series was conceived as a collection of sets of books covering popular chronological periods in British history, such as 'The Tudors' and 'the nineteenth century', together with the histories of other countries, such as France, Germany, Russia and the USA. This arrangement complemented the way in which early-modern and modern history has traditionally been taught in sixth forms, colleges and universities. In recent years, however, other ways of dividing up the past have become increasingly popular. In particular, there has been a greater emphasis on studying relatively brief periods in considerable detail and on comparing similar historical phenomena in different countries. These developments have generated a demand for appropriate learning materials, and, in response, two new 'strands' are being added to the main series - *In Depth* and *Themes*. The new volumes build directly on the features that have made *Access to History* so popular.

To the general reader

Although *Access* books have been specifically designed to meet the needs of examination students, these volumes also have much to offer the general reader. *Access* authors are committed to the belief that good history must not only be accurate, up-to-date and scholarly, but also clearly and attractively written. The main body of the text (excluding the 'Study Guides') should, therefore, form a readable and engaging survey of a topic. Moreover, each author has aimed not merely to provide as clear an explanation as possible of what happened in the past but also to stimulate readers and to challenge them into thinking for themselves about the past and its significance. Thus, although no prior knowledge is expected from the reader, he or she is treated as an intelligent and thinking person throughout. The author tends to share ideas and explore possibilities, instead of delivering so-called 'historical truths' from on high.

To the student reader

It is intended that *Access* books should be used by students studying history at a higher level. Its volumes are all designed to be working texts, which should be reasonably clear on a first reading but which will benefit from re-reading and close study. To be an effective and successful student, you need to budget your time wisely. Hence you should think carefully about how important the material in a particular book is for you. If you simply need to acquire a general grasp of a topic, the following approach will probably be effective:

  1. Read Chapter 1, which should give you an overview of the whole book, and think about its contents.

2. Skim through Chapter 2, paying particular attention to the opening section and to the headings and sub-headings. Decide if you need to read the whole chapter.
3. If you do, read the chapter, stopping at the end of every sub-division of the text to make notes.
4. Repeat stage 2 (and stage 3 where appropriate) for the other chapters.

If, however, your course - and your particular approach to it - demands a detailed knowledge of the contents of the book, you will need to be correspondingly more thorough. There is no perfect way of studying, and it is particularly worthwhile experimenting with different styles of note-making to find the one that best suits you. Nevertheless, the following plan of action is worth trying:

1. Read a whole chapter quickly, preferably at one sitting. Avoid the temptation - which may be very great - to make notes at this stage.
2. Study the flow diagram at the end of the chapter, ensuring that you understand the general 'shape' of what you have read.
3. Re-read the chapter more slowly, this time taking notes. You may well be amazed at how much more intelligible and straightforward the material seems on a second reading - and your notes will be correspondingly more useful to you when you have to write an essay or revise for an exam. In the long run, reading a chapter twice can, in fact, often save time. Be sure to make your notes in a clear, orderly fashion, and spread them out so that, if necessary, you can later add extra information.
4. Read the advice on essay questions, and do tackle the specimen titles. (Remember that if learning is to be effective, it must be active. No one - alas - has yet devised any substitute for real effort. It is up to you to make up your own mind on the key issues in any topic.)
5. Attempt the source-based questions. The guidance on tackling these exercises, which is generally given at least once in a book, is well worth reading and thinking about.

When you have finished the main chapters, go through the 'Further Reading' section. Remember that no single book can ever do more than introduce a topic, and it is to be hoped that - time permitting - you will want to read more widely. If *Access* books help you to discover just how diverse and fascinating the human past can be, the series will have succeeded in its aim - and you will experience that enthusiasm for the subject which, along with efficient learning, is the hallmark of all the best students.

Robert Pearce

Acknowledgements

The publishers would like to thank the following for their permission to use copyright illustrations:

The picture on the front cover is reproduced courtesy of Weidenfeld and Nicolson. David King Collection pp 22 and 102; Canning House Library, London p 55; Institut Amatller d'Art Hispanic pp 79, 104 and 119; photo by Agusti Centelles © DACS, 1998 p 87.

The publishers would like to thank the following for permission to reproduce material in the volume:

Addison Wesley Longman for extracts from *Spain's Civil War* by Harry Browne (1996); Allen & Unwin for an extract from *The Making of the Second World War* by A. Adamthwaite (1977); Faber & Faber Ltd for an extract from *Crusade in Spain by Jason Gurney* (1974) and for an extract from 'Spain 1937' by W.H. Auden which was reprinted from *The English Auden: Poems, Essays and Dramatic Writings 1927-1939*, edited by E. Mendelson; Victor Gollancz for an extract from *What I saw in Spain* by Leah Manning (1935); Macmillan for an extract from 'Volunteer in Trouble' by T.A.R. Hyndman which was reprinted from *The Distant Drums: Reflections on the Spanish Civil War* edited by Philip Toynbee; an extract from *The Times* 28 April 1937, © Times Newspapers Limited, 1937; an extract from *The Spanish Revolution: The Left and the Struggle for Power During the Civil War* by Burnett Bolloten, copyright © 1979 by the University of North Carolina Press, used by permission of the publisher.

Every effort has been made to trace and acknowledge ownership of copyright. The publishers will be glad to make any suitable arrangements with copyright holders whom it has not been possible to contact.

1 The Spanish Civil War – an Introduction

Early in July 1936 an aircraft was chartered from Olley Air Services in Croydon by Luis Bolín, who was the London correspondent of a right-wing Spanish newspaper. The purpose was to fly General Francisco Franco from the Canary Islands (where he was the Governor) to the Spanish colony of Morocco. There he was to lead a military rising against the elected Spanish government. The flight was disguised as a holiday trip, hence passengers had to be carried. This account by an English journalist, who assisted Bolín, conveys the surprisingly amateurish way in which the arrangements were made for this dangerous enterprise:

1　It was in July when Luis Bolín rang up and asked me to lunch. We lunched at Simpsons and de la Cierva (a Spaniard with aircraft expertise), completed the party. We began with appropriate gestures of conspiracy. We must have a quiet table. By the time Bolín and de la
5　Cierva after much whispering had rejected every vacant table in the room, hardly anyone could have been unaware of our pressing need for privacy.

　　We had begun to eat and as the atmosphere then was less electric I thought it would be safe to broach the subject of our meeting. And then
10　it happened. 'I want a man and three platinum blondes to fly to Africa tomorrow.' 'Must there really be three?' I asked and at that Bolín turned triumphantly to de la Cierva. 'I told you he would manage it!' 'Well probably two would be enough,' Bolín said regretfully, 'but of course the man must have had some experience; there might be trouble.'
15　After all the job was Pollard's by rights for he had experience of Moroccan, Mexican and Irish revolutions, and of course this meant war and he knew Spain. I telephoned him and asked, 'Can you fly to Africa tomorrow with two girls?' and heard the expected reply, 'depends upon the girls!' [1]

Franco finally arrived in Morocco on 19 July to an enthusiastic reception from the Army of Africa. The rising had already begun there and in many parts of mainland Spain. But what was intended to be a successful coup turned instead into a civil war which lasted almost three years, involved all the other major European powers and which still 'sells books and fills lecture halls.'[2] The war resulted from Spanish problems but it generated tremendous interest throughout the rest of Europe, not only because it was the only civil war to occur in a European state for many decades, but because it encapsulated the ideological struggle between democracy and fascism which dominated the 1930s.

　　The war can be seen as a precursor to the Second World War or even as the Second World War in miniature. Spaniards experienced all the horrors of modern warfare, albeit on a small scale, including air raids and terror bombing (as in the destruction of the Basque town of Guernica), and the wholesale killing of civilians who found themselves on the wrong side. But in other respects the fighting more resembled that of the First World War, with much of it consisting of static trench warfare along a 2,000 kilometre front where nothing might happen for months at a time, as described by George Orwell (an English writer who fought for the Republic) in this extract:

1   Up here in the hills round Saragossa it was simply the mingled boredom and discomfort of stationary warfare ... On every hill-top, Fascist or Loyalist, a knot of ragged, dirty men, shivering round their flag and trying to keep warm. And all day and night meaningless bullets wandering
5   across the empty valleys and only by some rare, improbable chance getting home on a human body. [3]

The war evoked passionate debate, not least among writers, novelists and poets, almost all of whom sided with the Republic. It was one of the first wars to be extensively covered by journalists. Many prominent literary figures, such as Ernest Hemingway, flocked to Spain to witness it at first hand or to fight for the Republic in the International Brigades. British writers who fought in the war included George Orwell, Julian Bell, who was a member of the intellectual 'Bloomsbury Set' and the nephew of the novelist Virginia Woolf, and the poets W.H Auden and John Cornford.

These verses from Auden's 'Spain', written in 1937, are an example of the poetry inspired by the war:

1   'What's your proposal? To build the just city? I will.
    I agree. Or is it the suicide pact, the romantic
    Death? Very well, I accept, for
    I am your choice, your decision. Yes, I am Spain' ...
5   To-morrow for the young the poets exploding like bombs,
    The walks by the lake, the weeks of perfect communion;
    To-morrow the bicycle races
    Through suburbs on Summer evenings. But to-day the struggle. [4]

Poets and authors alike felt so strongly about Spain because they were convinced that if fascism were to win then intellectual freedom itself would be destroyed. 'We were obsessed by the feeling that this was the supreme cause of our time ... And that unless ... fascism was defeated, we would be unable to exist as writers.'[5] Writers were, however, only a minority of those who fought for the Republic. Many ordinary working-class people from a variety of European countries enlisted in the International Brigades, and many more who stayed at home were involved in publicity and fund-raising.

The sections below provide an introduction to the events of the war and identify the issues to be explored in depth in the ensuing chapters.

1 The Causes of the War

No account of the Spanish Civil War is complete without an analysis of its causes. The immediate reasons for the outbreak of war can be located in the events of the Second Republic between 1931 and 1936, but its long-term origins have their roots in economic and social conflicts which date back to the nineteenth century.

Spanish society in the early twentieth century was characterised by extremes of wealth and poverty. Late economic development meant that agriculture was still the main occupation and industry was largely confined to Catalonia and the northern provinces. Economic and political power rested with the landowners, the Catholic Church and the army.

When a Spanish army was defeated in Morocco in 1921, the ensuing political crisis resulted in the dictatorship of Miguel Primo de Rivera which lasted until 1930. After Primo's fall, political unrest forced the abdication of the King, Alfonso XIII, in April 1931. Spain then became a Republic and the new government, a coalition of liberals and progressives, introduced a series of far-reaching reforms with the intention of redressing some of the social imbalances.

These reforms met with great hostility, not least from the church and property owners whose interests they threatened. To oppose them, an umbrella right-wing opposition party, the CEDA, was established which won the November 1933 elections to the Cortes (parliament). The next two years saw a determined effort to reverse reform. This in turn provoked an anarchist and Socialist rising in the Asturias coal-fields in northern Spain in October 1934, which was put down with great ferocity. Meantime a Spanish fascist party, the Falange, had emerged, though at the beginning of 1936 it was insignificant in numbers and influence.

In February 1936 the political pendulum swung back again when the Cortes election was won by a coalition of liberals and Socialists. But under this government the problems of the Republic intensified and the divisions in Spanish society became even more irreconcilable. The right wing, and especially the army, became convinced that the Republic could, and should, be destroyed by force. Hence, a number of generals engaged in secret plans for a military coup which was put into effect with the rising of July 1936.

Since this rising was only partially successful, it left Spain, by August 1936, almost equally divided between the Republican government and their opponents, who became known as the Nationalists.

2 The Events of the War from 1936 to 1939

a) The military events

The military history of the war consists mainly of a description of

Nationalist gains. Up to March 1937 it was dominated by the Nationalists' efforts to capture Madrid, the capital. When this failed, Franco turned his attention to the easier target of northern Spain, which was cut off from the rest of the Republic (see the map on page 82 in Chapter 6). Here, the Nationalist advance was swift, and by August 1937 all of the north had been captured. Then in February 1938 the Nationalists achieved a crucial breakthrough in central Spain. They reached the Mediterranean in April, and cut the Republican zone in half (see the map on page 90 in Chapter 6). From this point on they were certain of eventual success, though the war dragged on for another year before ending with a Nationalist victory in March 1939.

The outcome of the war was partly determined by the effectiveness with which both sides succeeded in organising and deploying their armed forces, and here the Nationalists proved to have the advantage. Foreign intervention was also very important. To further their own diplomatic ends, both Nazi Germany and Fascist Italy aided the Nationalists, while the Soviet Union sent aircraft, tanks and advisors to the Republic, which was also assisted by the International Brigades. But the Republic certainly received less aid than its opponents and was disadvantaged by the British and French policy of non-intervention.

b) The political events

These are as significant as the military events in explaining why the Nationalists won. At the start, both sides encompassed a variety of political groups, but it was the Nationalists who were most successful in enforcing unity.

The political and social situation in the Republic was complicated. In the summer of 1936 many regions, especially Catalonia, experienced a social and economic revolution, led by the anarchists. Owners of land and industry lost their property, which was collectivised or nationalised. But this revolution was opposed by Soviet advisors and Spanish Communists who wished to present Spain to the outside world as a moderate democracy. In May 1937 fighting broke out in Barcelona between the Communists and their more left-wing opponents, the anarchists and anti-Stalinist Marxists. The Communists won, but the legacy was lasting bitterness.

In the Nationalist zone, on the other hand, a unified military and political leadership under General Franco was quickly established by October 1937. The Nationalists could not avoid their own political crisis since Franco faced opposition both from the Carlists, a group wishing to restore the descendant of Don Carlos, a nineteenth-century pretender, to the throne, and from the Spanish fascists, the Falange. But in April 1937 he was able to exploit the Falange's internal conflicts and merge it with other groups under his own leadership. For the rest of the war Franco was not seriously challenged and he was able to successfully control, and play off against one another, the different factions on whom his regime rested.

3 Interpretations and Controversies

Most historical writing about the Civil War has, understandably, been favourable to the Republic. Early accounts tended to place the war in a European rather than a Spanish context, viewing it primarily as an example of the ideological conflicts of the 1930s. Within this perspective, the role of foreign powers - Germany, Italy, the Soviet Union, and of the International Brigades - was inevitably exaggerated.

This view of the war has been modified, and it is now more usual to regard it as essentially a Spanish affair, fought mainly by Spaniards, with its origins in Spanish history. It can be seen as the outcome of a hundred years of struggle between the forces of reaction and reform and the uprising as the last of a long line of army coups stretching back through the nineteenth century. The passage of time and the restoration of democracy in Spain since Franco's death in 1975 has enabled the war to be set in a wider context.

The emphasis has also moved away from general histories towards more detailed studies of particular aspects of the war. Many more Spanish sources have become available in the last 20 years. More regard is now paid to social and economic factors and to oral history. While the bias is still towards the Republic, there is a more objective approach with greater emphasis on Republican miscalculations, both military and political. Events in Nationalist Spain and the role of Franco, the Falange and the Carlists have all merited more attention, as have developments in Spain since 1975.

The war has always been a subject of controversy. There are three main areas of dispute among historians. Firstly, why did a civil war break out and who was to blame for this? Why could Spaniards not reconcile their differences short of going to war and at what point did the conflict become inevitable? Responsibility for the war has usually been held to lie with the right wing, who did not scruple to resort to force to prevent reasonable reforms. However, some authors are now more critical of the role of the Republic in helping bring about the conflict.

A second equally contentious question is why the Nationalists managed to win the war. They started with some serious disadvantages, not least that they were rebelling against a democratically elected government and that their coup had failed in most major Spanish cities. Yet, a year later in the Summer of 1937, they had made significant gains and by early 1938 were clearly winning.

It used to be assumed that Nationalist success was very largely, if not wholly, due to the substantial aid they received from Germany and Italy, in contrast with the more limited Soviet help received by the

Republic. This explanation is now regarded as simplistic. Greater attention is now paid to military organisation and tactics. More research has been carried out on the economic and financial factors which favoured the Nationalists. Also, the politics of the two zones are now seen as important in explaining success or failure. Nationalist Spain under Franco was undisputedly a more cohesive society than the Republic, which remained a battleground of conflicting ideologies.

A related issue to this argument is the role of the Communist Party in the Republic. Did the Communists undermine the Republic, or did they help it survive as long as it did against overwhelming odds? This debate too has gone through various permutations. Earlier books tended to take a pro-Communist line but the arguments are now more balanced in favour of other left-wing groups.

The third area of controversy is the relationship between Nationalist Spain and fascism. Was Franco's Spain a fascist dictatorship along the lines of Mussolini's Italy, or merely a conventional military regime of the type which Spain had periodically experienced in the preceding hundred years? This debate centres on Franco and his political ideas, on the role and views of the Falange and other Nationalist political groups and also, of course, on the meaning of the term 'fascism'. At first sight it seems that Nationalist Spain was not fascist. Far from possessing a fascist ideology, Franco had few political ideas and little sympathy with the Falange. The Falange itself, the only genuine fascist party in Spain, attracted little support prior to the outbreak of the war and, after a brief resurgence, fell under Franco's control in April 1937. However, the debate does not end there: the characteristics and roles of other right-wing groups and the similarities between Spain, Italy and Germany also have to be considered.

These issues, together with the events of the war, are comprehensively covered in the chapters which follow.

References
1   D. Jerrold, *Georgian Adventure* (Collins, 1937), pp.369-70
2   Paul Preston, *The politics of revenge, fascism and the military in 20th century Spain* (Routledge, 1990), p.34.
3   George Orwell, *Homage to Catalonia* (Secker & Warburg, 1970), pp.29-40.
4   Quoted in Valentine Cunningham (ed), *Spanish front, writers on the Civil War* (Oxford University Press, 1986), pp. 3-4.
5   Stephen Spender speaking in an ITV series, *The Spanish Civil War*, programme 3, 'Battleground for idealists', 1982.

Summary Diagram
The Spanish Civil War - an Introduction

The causes of the war

↓

1898 to 1931

Economic problems   Social problems   Political problems   Imperial problems

↓

The Second Republic 1931 to 1936

Church, land and   Right-wing reaction   The Popular Front
Army reforms   The Asturias Rising   and social unrest

↓

The Rising, July 1936

↓

The War, July 1936 to March 1939

Military tactics   Foreign involvement   Political developments in
Armies and militias   Germany, Italy, USSR   Republican and
                                                               Nationalist Spain

↘   ↓   ↙

Nationalist success, March

Issues and controversies

↙   ↓   ↘

Why did civil war break out?   **Why did the Nationalists win?**
Did responsibility lie wholly   Foreign aid?
with the right?   Military factors?
Was war inevitable?   Political factors?

Was Franco's regime fascist?
What were Franco's political views?
How important was the Falange?
What were the similarities and differences
between Nationalist Spain and Italy/Germany?

2 Spain from 1898 to 1936

1 Economic Problems and Social Conflicts

The Civil War had its origins in economic and social problems. In the first decades of the twentieth century, Spain was still a predominantly agricultural country and more than half the employed population worked on the land. In southern Spain, in the provinces of Andalusia and Extremadura, semi-feudal conditions prevailed on the large estates (latifundia), where labourers were paid starvation wages and poverty and illiteracy were rife. (See the map on page 9.) On the other hand in northern Spain the typical farm was owned or rented by peasant proprietors. Rents were high and smallholdings often too tiny to generate a reasonable living, but there were clear differences between the interests of small farmers and those of landless labourers who more resembled a rural working class than a peasantry.

Though Spain had long-standing commercial links with the rest of Europe, there was little industrial development before the mid-nineteenth century. Industrialisation was still at an early stage of development in the 1930s. The main industrial regions were Catalonia, where textile and shipping industries had grown up around the port of Barcelona, the coal mining areas of the Asturias, and the Basque country, where iron, steel and engineering had developed. In the absence of a strong industrial base, emigration, mainly to the former Spanish colonies in South America, had served to alleviate the pressures of population growth, but, after the First World War, tighter immigration controls reduced these opportunities, resulting in more migrants from rural areas flooding into the towns and a consequent increase in housing and other social problems.

Institutions such as the Catholic Church and the army were extremely influential. Though the numbers of practising Catholics were diminishing, Spain was still a religious country and the Church had long occupied a privileged position. The Concordat of 1851 made Catholicism the official religion and guaranteed the clergy a state-financed income, thus ensuring Church support for the state. The Church almost always supported the interests of the wealthier classes, and its outdated political attitudes are illustrated in this extract from a Catechism of 1927:

> What kind of sin is committed by one who votes for a liberal candidate?
> Generally a mortal sin.
> Is it a sin for a Catholic to read a liberal newspaper?
> He may read the Stock Exchange News.[1]

The reactionary views of the hierarchy and most of the clergy led to hatred and resentment of the Church by many poorer Spaniards, and the burning of churches and convents became a familiar feature of

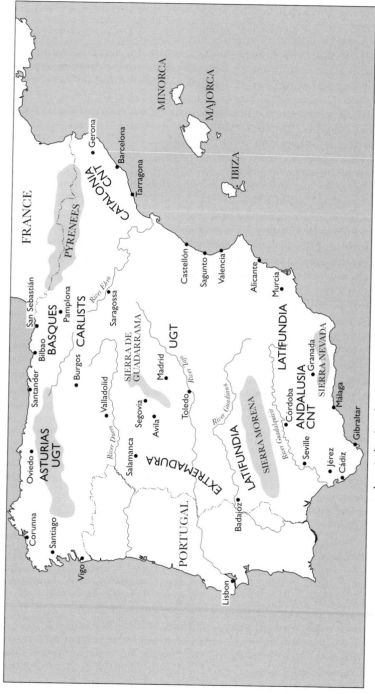

A map showing the regions and political groups within Spain

disturbances in urban Spain. At the same time there was a growth of anti-clericalism among the more radical middle class.

The army was another important institution. By the early twentieth century it was far too large and expensive for Spain's diminished world role and was top heavy with officers - one for every nine men. But it was almost impossible for governments to reduce, reform or disregard it, since, besides providing employment for the upper and middle class, the army symbolised Spain's former greatness. It was a Spanish tradition for generals and other officers to take political initiatives and inaugurate coups or *pronunciamientos* and, although the last of these had occurred in 1874, the army still had the potential to destroy or create governments.

Spain's late industrial development meant that the Spanish middle class remained small. It was also divided between the wealthier commercial and industrial classes, who identified with the views and aspirations of the landed class, and professional men, owners of small businesses and shopkeepers, who tended to be more radical.

With the growth of industry there emerged a working class and a labour movement divided between Socialists and anarchists. A Socialist Party (PSOE from its Spanish initials) had been formed in 1879. Like most other European Socialist parties of the time it was revolutionary in theory but in practice generally pursued its aims through parliamentary channels, though with little success before 1931. In the 1920s it was led by Largo Caballero, a former plasterer and trade union official, and Indalecio Prieto, a journalist and member of the Cortes. A Socialist trade union, the UGT, was established in 1882 and was strongest in Madrid among craftsmen such as printers, in the Basque country and in the mining districts of the Asturias. Both the PSOE and the UGT grew rapidly in the years of industrial expansion just before and during the First World War. In the early 1920s, when the PSOE split over whether to support the 1917 Bolshevik Revolution, a Spanish Communist Party was formed. However, by the beginning of the 1930s the Communists were a small and relatively unimportant group.

The main competition to the Socialists came from the anarchists and their union, the CNT, which had been set up in 1911 and was particularly well-supported by workers in Catalonia and peasants and labourers in Andalusia. Spain was unusual in Europe in having a strong anarchist movement, which had taken root in the 1870s when Bakunin, one of the founders of the movement, had visited the country. The anarchists gained support through their advocacy of land reform, which appealed to the rural labourers, and their promotion of revolutionary solutions, which was attractive in a country where the ability to effect change through legal means was very limited. Anarchists aimed to destroy the state by means of a spontaneous revolution or a political general strike, and to establish a new society based on self-governing communities. They had no faith in parliamentary methods and refused to participate in elections. Extreme anarchists resorted to bomb throwing and attempted assassinations, via secret terrorist societies such as the FAI (from its initials), formed in 1927.

With Spanish society sharply polarised between the wealthy upper class on the one hand and the mass of peasants and urban workers on the other, unrest frequently erupted in rioting and disturbances. Workers and peasants increasingly clashed with the Civil Guard, a much hated armed police force. In the early twentieth century, Barcelona, with its explosive mix of anarchism, strikes and Catalan nationalism, was described as 'the most turbulent city in Europe'.[2] There, in the so-called 'Tragic Week' in the Summer of 1909, many people were killed in a spate of rioting and church burning occasioned by the calling up of reservists for the Moroccan War.

2 Spanish Politics from 1898 to 1923

Spain in 1898 was a constitutional monarchy. The King had some prerogatives, but power mainly resided in parliament, the Cortes. Universal male suffrage had been introduced in the 1880s, but Spain was far from being a genuine democracy and more resembled an oligarchy with professional politicians alternating in government. The *Caciquismo* system ensured that elections were managed and controlled by local notables, the caciques, by means of bribery, intimidation, ballot rigging or patronage. From the 1870s Spanish political life revolved around the alternation in power (the *Turno*) of Conservatives and Liberals, most governments being coalitions or permutations of the main interest groups. Modern party structures hardly existed, though after 1900 Socialist and Republican organisations began to appear in the larger towns. There were few significant differences between the two main parties and local government was usually characterised by the same corruption as prevailed in national politics. The great majority of Spaniards therefore had little experience of political activity and did not feel that the existing parties represented their interests. The system bred cynicism, apathy and disillusionment similar to that found in Italy after 1870.

Dissatisfaction with central government was compounded in Catalonia and the Basque region, by the emergence of separatist movements. In these regions a distinct language, culture and economy gave rise during the nineteenth century to demands for self-government within the Spanish state, aspirations opposed by governments in Madrid. Catalan nationalism was the most active at this time, promoted first by the Lliga, a mainly conservative party, and from the 1920s by the more radical Esquerra led by Luis Companys.

Spain had long since relinquished most of her empire in Central and South America but in 1898 her prestige suffered another devastating blow when, following a war with the United States, she lost most of her remaining colonies, including Cuba and the Philippines. This humiliating defeat demoralised the armed forces and graphically demonstrated Spain's decline to the status of a third rate power. A contemporary view expressed this malaise: 'All is broken down in this wretched country; no government, no elections, no parties, no navy, no army. All is ruin, decadence.'[3]

Between 1898 and 1923 the regime stumbled from crisis to crisis. Sporadic attempts were made to make the parliamentary system more effective, to 'regenerate' it in the vocabulary of the day, but all these efforts floundered. Alfonso XIII, who became King in 1885, was superficially a modern monarch with an interest in motor cars and technology, but he had no real desire for change and upheld established institutions. One of few concessions to be made was limited self-government for Catalonia in 1913 but this did not appease most Catalan nationalists.

In 1906 Spain had an opportunity to partly resurrect her former imperial greatness, when a part of Morocco was acquired by agreement with France. But Morocco proved difficult to pacify. From 1906 to 1926 a series of campaigns had to be undertaken against the Rif tribes, initially with little success. The Moroccan Wars provided a *raison d'être* for the army and promoted the emergence of a cohesive and experienced breed of army officers, the Africanistas, of whom General Franco was a good example, but the casualty rate was high and conscription met with considerable opposition.

Spain was neutral during the First World War and at first this boosted the economy, which was temporarily freed from foreign competition. Industry prospered, as Spain supplied France with textiles and other goods. However, the boom was short-lived. The end of the war brought renewed competition, unemployment and a fall in demand for Spain's agricultural exports. Even during the war a political crisis had erupted. Starting in the summer of 1917 with a group of army officers protesting at low pay, it escalated to include the Catalan separatists, the trade unions and the anarchists. An 'Assembly Movement' met in Barcelona to demand a new constitution and Catalan autonomy. The crisis fizzled out, but the end of war brought renewed industrial unrest. Between 1918 and 1921 Barcelona was the scene of terrorism and gun battles between the CNT and the employers, in which over 1,000 people died.

The final blow to the credibility of the regime came in July 1921 when the Rif leader, Abd el Krim, defeated a Spanish force in Morocco at the Battle of Anual. More than 10,000 Spanish troops were killed. A Parliamentary Committee was set up to investigate responsibility for the disaster. To forestall its report, which it was thought might blame the King and precipitate the downfall of the monarchy, the military governor of Barcelona, General Miguel Primo de Rivera, declared a *pronunciamiento* in September 1923. He called for Spain to be governed by patriots rather than politicians. Alfonso thankfully asked him to form a government.

3 The Dictatorship of Primo de Rivera, 1923 to 1930

Primo came to power as a result of accumulated political and social problems, of which the defeat in Morocco was the last straw. Described by the King as 'My Mussolini' (a reference to the Italian dictator whom Alfonso admired), Primo suspended the Constitution, closed the Cortes and banned political parties, setting up instead a Directory of Generals to run the government. His political ideas were few and his policies mainly pragmatic. He liked to think of himself as a benevolent despot, a man of action who possessed an intuitive feel for the will of the people. He attempted to fill the political vacuum by setting up his own political party, the Patriotic Union, but it did not thrive. Primo claimed that he eventually intended to restore 'normal' political life but the opportune moment to do so never arrived.

Up to 1929 Primo's regime coincided with a period of relative economic prosperity and he had some achievements to his credit including winning the support of the Socialists and the UGT. In 1926 he introduced a system of arbitration in labour disputes with UGT participation. He succeeded in exacerbating the rivalry between the Socialists and anarchists by conciliating the former while persecuting the latter. Primo also did his best to modernise the economy by state intervention. He embarked on a programme of public works, including roads, hydro-electric schemes, irrigation schemes and public buildings. The 1924 Municipal Statute empowered local authorities to borrow money for urban improvements. Several new banks were created to promote credit. There was some investment in the railways, which were badly underfunded, and foreign trade increased. By 1926 the war in Morocco was finally won, albeit with French assistance.

But Primo's government also failed in many respects. Calvo Sotelo, the Finance Minister, was capable, but could not reform the tax system. Public works could therefore only be financed by budget deficits or loans. In 1928 the peseta (whose exchange rate was symbolic of the standing of the regime) fell in value. There was opposition to the monopolies Primo had granted for the sale of petrol and Moroccan tobacco. He did not tackle land reform. Censorship of the press and restrictions on freedom of speech roused opposition, as did the abolition of concessions to Catalonia and the prohibition of the official use of the Catalan language.

The prosperity of the 1920s which was partly due to a world-wide boom, collapsed in the Great Depression of 1929. Spain, with a large agricultural self-employed sector and protected behind high tariff barriers, was less affected by the depression than many other countries. Nevertheless, it was impossible to entirely escape its effects. Agriculture suffered as food prices fell, and unemployment increased.

Primo's downfall, however, was due less to the depression than to his failure to reconcile a variety of important interest groups. The politicians who had lost influence under his regime were antagonised while, at the same time, Republicanism gained ground with demands that the constitution be re-introduced. In particular, he made the fatal mistake of offending the army by changing the promotion system in the prestigious artillery corps and eventually closing it down entirely. The King, some of whose powers had also been curtailed, gradually turned against him. In January 1930 the regime ground to a halt and Primo resigned and went into self-imposed exile in France, where he died shortly afterwards.

4 The Establishment of the Second Republic

After the fall of Primo, Spain, according to his successor General Berenguer, was 'like a bottle of champagne about to blow its cork.'[4] Berenguer's rule was brief and neither he nor Admiral Aznar, who succeeded him, could form a viable government. Had a democratic constitution been restored in 1930, the monarchy might just have survived, but by 1931 it was too late. Alfonso's position had been thoroughly undermined since he was closely associated with the unpopularity of Primo's regime, which he himself had placed in power.

There was also steadily growing support for a republic, which was increasingly seen as the only form of government which would introduce the reforms necessary to drag Spain into the twentieth century. In August 1930 representatives of Republicans, Liberals and Catalans, later joined by the Socialists, had met at San Sebastian to sign a secret pact to overthrow the monarchy. The coming together of these formerly disparate political groups spelt the end for Alfonso.

To test opinion, the King agreed to hold municipal elections on 12 April 1931, but the results were devastating for the monarchy, with a republican triumph in the towns, though not in the countryside. Two days later the King left Spain, though wishing to keep all his options open he merely 'suspended the use of his prerogative' instead of abdicating outright. Significantly, the army, smarting from Primo's slights, refused to support Alfonso, a 'negative *pronunciamiento*' as it was described. The speedy and relatively smooth transition of power from monarchy to Republic is described in this eyewitness account, which illustrates the reluctance of the politicians to support Alfonso, and also the enthusiasm which greeted the new regime:

1 Negotiations [for the future of the monarchy] were carried on in the salon of the house of a close personal friend of the monarch. Alcala

Zamora [one of the main Republicans] was quite adamant: 'the King must leave before sunset.' The King walked out into an ante-chamber
5 where various Cabinet Ministers, grandees and other personalities were gathered. A dashing cavalry officer, General Marquess of Cavalcanti, said, 'Sire I offer you the full support of my troops to defend your throne'. General Berenguer immediately cut in with a sharp, 'Prove what you say;
10 prove that it is possible to restore order by bringing out troops before making such sweeping statements'. Cavalcanti was about to answer back angrily but Don Alfonso intervened sadly saying, 'There is no need at all for discussion, my friends, my mind is quite made up and I shall leave the country tonight' … Shortly before dusk five or six powerful cars swung
15 out of the private entrance to the palace grounds and twelve hours later the King was sailing for Marseilles on the cruiser *Jaime I*.

   While Don Alfonso was sadly deciding which way to leave, Sr Alcala Zamora and his colleagues set out for the Ministry of the Interior. Their cars wedged their way through the delirious crowds at a speed which
20 would make snails' pace seem like the Grand Prix in comparison … Civil Guards swung back the doors and Zamora and his friends were swept up the stairs on a tidal wave of enthusiastic supporters. The key ministry was in Republican hands without a drop of blood being shed.[5]

5 The Second Republic, April 1931 to February 1936

At first, there was enormous support for the new government. It was not the first time there had been a republic in Spain (there had been an earlier brief First Republic in the 1870s), but the Second Republic implied not only political, but also social, change. However, in implementing reforms the Republic would have to reconcile widely conflicting interests and meet the demands of its working-class and peasant supporters without incurring too much hostility from the upper and middle classes. In practice this proved impossible, and expectations were raised which could not be satisfied.

a) The Left Republic, April 1931 to November 1933

The elections to the Cortes were held in June 1931. The new electoral system favoured coalitions and blocs by providing that the list of candidates which won over 50 per cent of vote in any province would get 80 per cent of the seats. Small majorities in elections were therefore translated into large majorities in the Cortes. Such right-wing parties as there were had fallen into disarray in the years of Primo's dictatorship, so that in 1931 victory went to the better organised Republican bloc, with the Socialists emerging as the single largest party, while the non-Republican Right won only 57 seats out of 473. The first Republican Government was a coalition, encompassing a wide political spectrum from liberal Catholics (who included the Prime Minister, Alcala Zamora), to Socialists. The cabinet included Radicals (originally reformers, but by 1931 radical in name only), led by Lerroux, left-wing Republicans led by Azaña and three Socialists.

The new Government embarked on a series of ambitious reforms. Its first task was to draw up a new Constitution. This was finally agreed in December 1931 and declared Spain to be 'a democratic Republic of workers of all classes'. Article 44 posed a potential threat to property rights by allowing confiscation of property for reasons of 'social utility'. But the most controversial clauses concerned the Church: state support for the clergy was to end within two years and religious orders were excluded from education and were threatened with dissolution. Education was henceforth to be wholly secular and civil marriage and divorce were introduced. The religious clauses of the Constitution were opposed by Zamora and Maura, the Minister of the Interior, who both resigned in October 1931 and the composition of the government shifted to the left. Zamora became the President of the Republic but power now rested with the new Prime Minister, Azana, who was known for his strong anti-clerical views.

Many felt that the removal of Church privileges was long overdue, and some degree of anti-clericalism under the Republic was inevitable. It can be argued, however, that the Church reforms went too far. They mobilised not only the Church but also many Catholic Spaniards (including peasants) against the Republic and motivated the right wing to reorganise more quickly than might otherwise have been the case. Statements such as Azaña's provocative response to church burning - that 'all the convents in Madrid are not worth the life of a single republican' - were not calculated to reassure Spanish Catholics. Perhaps the Republic did not try sufficiently hard to conciliate the poorer clergy. However, given their social conservatism and the fact that the government was proposing to remove their state subsided salaries, it is unlikely that most of the clergy could ever have been reconciled to the Republic.

The government was also determined to deal with the army, which, in addition to posing a potential danger to the Republic, was regarded as expensive, wasteful and incompetent. In 1931 officers were offered the option of retirement on full pay, of which about half took advantage. Military academies, including Saragossa where Franco was in command, were closed and military promotions cancelled. These measures were more effective than earlier attempts at reform, but they did not resolve the army's relations with the Republic. It remained a powerful force and the hard-core of officers who remained tended to be the *Africanistas*, who had the most military experience but were also the most anti-Republican. A further reform was the creation, in October 1931, of a new internal police force, the Assault Guard, which it was hoped would support the Republic and act as a counterweight to the Civil Guard.

In 1932 a large degree of autonomy was granted to Catalonia. The Catalan parliament, the Generalitat, was given control over most domestic matters, though in some respects the boundary between regional and central authority was unclear. This committed most Catalans firmly to support of the Republic but was opposed by the right on the grounds that the unity of the Spanish state was being destroyed.

Together with the Church reforms, the most contentious area of the left Republic's work was land reform. Given the importance of land in the economy and the extent of rural poverty, which had been aggravated by the depression, this was the key to the success or failure of the Republic. The expectations of peasants and labourers were high and both the CNT and the UGT had gained support among agricultural labourers in the south. Land reform began in April 1931, when all leases were frozen and eviction was prohibited, except for non-payment of rent. Landowners were forbidden to allow land to go out of cultivation. The Law of Municipal Boundaries forbade the hiring of migrant labour while local workers were still unemployed: this prevented the traditional methods of strike breaking - bringing in outside labour or refusing the cultivate land. In addition there were arbitration committees (which built on those set up by Primo) to enforce labour legislation, such as the eight hour day, and to fix minimum wages.

The most controversial land measure was the Agrarian Reform Law of September 1932. It applied to the whole country and enabled the state to take over large estates and church land and to redistribute these to the peasants. In theory compensation was to be paid, but in practice there was little money available for this purpose. An Agrarian Reform Institute was to oversee the changes. Land which was redistributed technically belonged to the state but could be worked as private plots or in collective farms, and great debate ensued over the merits or otherwise of collectivisation versus individual ownership. However, the Act, disparaged by Largo Caballero as 'an aspirin to cure appendicitis', proved disappointing since little land in fact changed hands. The measure was riddled with loopholes and was difficult to interpret, and only about 7,000 families had been settled on confiscated estates by 1933. A deficiency of this reform was that it focused on the issue of ownership and failed to deal with the equally basic problems of rural indebtedness and lack of investment to improve productivity.

There was indeed little public finance available for economic improvements of any kind. The ability of the Republic to deliver on reform was restricted by the depression and shortage of revenue from taxes, a result of the inefficient and inequitable tax system. Prieto, the Finance Minister, followed the traditional financial strategy of cutting expenditure and balancing the budget (a course of action taken also in Britain, Weimar Germany and France during the depression), and there was no real effort to make the tax system fairer or to redistribute wealth.

Though land reform was ineffective it succeeded in alarming not only landowners but small peasant proprietors and the property owning classes generally, since it was seen as a precursor to a general attack on property rights and made it appear that Spain was moving in the direction of revolution on the Soviet model. On the other hand, workers and rural labourers were highly dissatisfied with the slow pace of change. The anarchists had never had any faith in the Republic and promoted strikes and risings. Increasing clashes between the peasants and the Civil Guard demonstrated the extent to which the Republic was losing control of events in rural Spain. Serious incidents occurred in December 1931 at Castilblanco in Extremadura, where four Civil guards were killed by peasants after they tried to break up a demonstration, and in January 1933 in Casas Viejas in southern Spain, where the Civil Guard killed several villagers.

The right was as antagonised as the left. There was a revival of the extreme monarchist right, the Carlists, who aimed to restore to the throne not Alfonso, but Don Carlos, the descendant of a 19th-century pretender. Carlism had its base in Navarre in northern Spain where peasants began joining its para-military groups, the *requetés*. The army was also hostile. In August 1932 General Sanjurjo attempted to over-throw the Republic by force with an army coup in Seville and Madrid. However, he did not obtain as much support as he expected, the coup failed and he was imprisoned and exiled to Portugal.

But the main challenge to the left Republic came not from Carlists nor the army but from what can be described as the 'legal' right. Right-wing parties hardly existed in April 1931, though the Catholic monar-chist papers *El Debate* and *ABC* provided a focal point for opposition. But the Church reforms prompted the emergence of groups such as *Acción Española* in 1931, *Acción Popular* in 1932 and, finally, in February 1933 the CEDA (Spanish Confederation of Autonomous Right-wing Groups) led by a lawyer Gil Robles. The CEDA was a right-wing umbrella organisation which stood for 'Accidentalism', meaning that it professed indifference to forms of government as long as Catholic interests were protected. Nominally the CEDA supported the repub-lican form of government, but its policies were ambiguous and often seemed anti-democratic. Gil Robles praised Hitler and Mussolini and visited Germany in 1933 to attend a Nuremberg rally. In these extracts from his speeches in 1933 he could appear to be endorsing fascism in his hostility to democracy, readiness to espouse violence and favourable references to Germany and to totalitarianism:

1 When the social order is threatened Catholics should unite to defend it and safeguard the principles of Christian civilisation ... we are faced with a social revolution; in the political panorama of Europe I can see only the formation of Marxist and anti-Marxist groups. This is what is
5 happening in Germany and in Spain also ... We must give Spain a true

unity, a new spirit, a totalitarian polity ... it is necessary now to defeat Socialism inexorably. We must found a new state, purge the fatherland of judaising freemasons ... What does it matter if we have to shed blood! We need full power and that is what we demand ... to realise 10 this ideal we are not going to waste time with archaic forms. Democracy is not an end but a means to the conquest of the new state. When the time comes either parliament submits or we will eliminate it ...[6]

Historians differ as to whether the CEDA can really be regarded as fascist. Paul Preston sees some continuity between the CEDA and Franco's regime, citing its aim of establishing an authoritarian corporate state on the lines of Mussolini's Italy. On the other hand, Sheelagh Ellwood considers that while 'Gil Robles had many of the traits of European fascism, such as its rabid anti-Marxism, its populism and a vociferous youth movements ... he was not, strictly speaking, a fascist for he was also a monarchist, a fervent Catholic and his message was reactionary not revolutionary'.[7] A genuine Spanish fascist movement, the Falange (see chapter 3), was in existence in 1933 but it was unimportant at this time compared with the CEDA.

b) The Right Republic, November 1933 to February 1936

In the Autumn of 1933 the CEDA got its opportunity when the government ran out of impetus and ideas. Azaña resigned and his successors both failed to form viable governments, and so an election was called for November 1933. This time the right benefited from the electoral system, winning a large majority of seats. They were well organised, whereas the Socialists refused to co-operate with the other Republican parties and the anarchists abstained. Women got the vote for the first time in Spain, which may have helped boost the conservative vote.

The elections ushered in what the left described as the *bienio negro* - the 'two black years', when the reforms of the previous two years were reversed, and socialism and anarchism were both suppressed. The CEDA, though the single largest party, did not take office - instead, Radical Governments under Lerroux and Samper continued, though now with a right-wing bias. Meantime, the Caballero wing of the Socialists, disillusioned with the ability of the Republic to implement reform and fearing a right-wing coup, became more revolutionary. As Prieto and his supporters continued to support parliamentary methods, a greater rift developed between the two rival Socialist leaders. It was inevitable that Spanish politics should be viewed in a European context. The Socialists were apprehensive of meeting the same fate as their colleagues in Germany, where Hitler had just come to power, or in Austria, where the socialists had recently been suppressed by the Dollfuss Government. Equally, the Spanish right was influenced by the example of Mussolini's apparently strong, successful rule in Italy. The *bienio negro* therefore saw a widening of the divisions between right and left, with the right fearing a Marxist revolution and the left a right-wing dictatorship.

Tension came to a head when three CEDA members finally entered the government in October 1934. The Socialists, who regarded the CEDA as fascist, called for a general strike, which was intended to be the precursor of a workers' rising. This was quickly put down in Madrid and Barcelona, but in the Asturias coalfield in northern Spain it was more successful, bringing together Socialists, the CNT and the Communists. After five days of fighting the miners captured Oviedo, the provincial capital, and established a commune.

This sympathetic account by an English journalist emphasises the relatively orderly characteristics of this rising:

1   It seems very certain that if he could have chosen, Largo Caballero would have preferred the strictly constitutional parliamentary way for he is a typical reformist leader ... Whether from conviction, expediency or from a natural desire to retain his influence with the rank and file
5   after the elections of 1933 he changed his political tactics. He was bitterly denouncing the sham, shadow institutions of democracy, declaring that if the Republic was to be saved, the road must be closed to fascism and that this would not be achieved by mere parliamentary action.
10   On the 4 October Lerroux announced that three fascists, the nominees of Gil Robles, had been taken into his new Cabinet. That evening the general strike began in the Asturias; it became almost immediately an armed rising ... In every section of the towns, in every village, Soviets of workers and peasants were formed.
15   Among the decrees passed were those abolishing private ownership of the means of production and abolishing rent. All communications were cut, the railway blockaded and Oviedo the government centre seized and held by the revolutionary forces. Oviedo possessed two large armaments factories. From this source the miners availed themselves of
20   20,000 rifles, hundreds of machine guns, several pieces of light artillery, some armoured cars and an armoured train. For nine days they held the town against the combined efforts of the military garrison, the civil guard and the assault guards and against the foreign legion and Arab army corps which had landed in Gijón and were advancing on the town
25   ... in Mieres [a mining village] the miners entered the village without firing a single shot and proclaimed a peasant and workers' government. The leaders gave out vouchers for the acquiring of provisions and shared them out among the inhabitants. Money was abolished and a Red Guard formed. The arsenal of arms was prepared in the church but they
30   did not do the slightest harm to the priest.'[8]

The Professor of Law at Oviedo University, however, took an opposite view:

1   The excuse to set the movement going was the solution announced for
     the ministerial crisis of the beginning of October ... Those who
     objected to the ministerial participation of Popular Action were the
     extreme left group, who had become enemies of the regime from the
5   moment when the republic ceased to obey their wishes.
         The Socialists since their fall from power had proclaimed themselves
     enemies of the 'bourgeois Republic' which they had supported in 1931.
     Now they hurled themselves against it with violence to conquer 'all
     power to the proletariat' by means of a bloody revolution.
10   The town of Oviedo was insufficiently garrisoned by less than 1,000
     men belonging to the army and the assault guards clumsily distributed
     over official centres and a few strategic points ... These dispositions
     permitted an avalanche of invaders, some 8,000 miners perfectly armed
     and using dynamite with skill and courage to seize most of the town on
15   the night of 5th October ... It was a very cruel battle ... more than 110
     houses, the finest in the town were burned or blown up, including build-
     ings such as the university (where in the destruction of its magnificent
     library the accumulated treasures of four centuries were lost) ... The
     civil population underwent all the horrors of war and revolution
20   combined ... Nine terrible days passed without light, without water,
     with scarcely any food ... Red Guards entered the houses through shat-
     tered doors or broken windows, molesting, imprisoning and shooting at
     pleasure. The greatest cruelty was shown to priests and nuns. About 40
     were killed in the Asturias.[9]

The Asturias rising was a watershed in the history of the Republic. It
was crushed with great harshness by the Foreign Legion and Moors,
with 4,000 casualties. Thousands were imprisoned or exiled,
including all the UGT and Socialist leaders. The defeat of the rising
and the consequent repression pushed Largo Caballero, 'the Spanish
Lenin', into a still more revolutionary stance, while at the same time
increasing the right's fear of Bolshevism. The Asturias rebellion therefore substantially increased the likelihood of civil war.

6 The Popular Front in Power, February to July 1936

By February 1936 Lerroux's Government was in difficulty, partly due
to his involvement in a series of financial scandals, and this initiated
new elections. In response to the *bienio negro*, the Republicans,
Socialists, Catalan left and the Communists had already met in 1935
to form a Popular Front against the right. Popular Fronts were
alliances of anti-fascist parties whose establishment in western
European states was being promoted by Stalin as a method of
combating fascism and of gathering support for the defence of Soviet
interests against the Nazi German threat.

The Spanish Popular Front programme in February 1936 was fairly innocuous, making few specific demands except for an amnesty for political prisoners and the reintroduction of some social legislation. The Communist Party Election Poster (see below) emphasises the unity of all the Popular Front parties, including their youth movements. The main figure represents ordinary Spaniards, upholding the Republic against the machinations of the Church and industrialists, while the slogans call for the release of political prisoners and provision of bread for the masses.

The monarchist and CEDA right warned of the likelihood of Communist revolution if the Front prevailed, but nevertheless it achieved a majority of seats in the election, though few of these were won by the Communist Party. The Socialists, however, disillusioned by

A Communist party poster tells people to vote for the Popular Front in the election of February, 1936

the limitations of the reforms of 1931 to 1933, refused to join Azaña's Popular Front government. This weakened the Government without strengthening the Socialists. The Caballero Socialists had no real plans for a revolution but they spoke as if they did, thus playing into the hands of the right, who claimed that Spain was sinking into chaos. Apart from releasing political prisoners, the Azaña government did little in practice to alarm the wealthier classes, but it could not prevent either the increasing polarisation of Spanish politics or the growing disorder in the country.

To what extent Spain was descending into violence during this period is debatable and certainly some of the disorder was promoted by the right and especially by the youth movements of the CEDA and Falange who engaged in street fighting with left-wing groups. But though the degree of the left-wing disorder was exaggerated, disturbances certainly increased. Largo Caballero made a series of inflammatory speeches. Peasants began to take direct action and occupy land, more of which was taken over in the Spring of 1936 than in the previous five years. In March, in Extremadura, 60,000 peasants joined forces to take over several estates while the police and army stood by. Other rural workers went on strike demanding higher wages, anarchist militias (para-military groups) were formed and many landowners fled to the cities.

Urban Spain also experienced severe disturbances. On 1 May, May Day, a general strike was called by the CNT. June saw strikes by building workers in Madrid and by such diverse groups as lift-workers, waiters and bull-fighters. In the few months of the Popular Front government over a hundred churches were destroyed throughout Spain and there were numerous bomb explosions and some assassination attempts. Meanwhile, extreme political groups gained increasing support.

Outright revolution was unlikely but, on the other hand, it was clear that law and order were gradually breaking down in some parts of Spain and that the government seemed powerless to prevent this. From May, when Casares Quiroga took over as Prime Minister, the government looked even weaker. Casares suffered from ill-health and did not provide any positive direction. It was in this situation, when the left were theorising about revolution, that the right began planning an actual counter-revolution.

7 Why did Both the Monarchy and the Republic Fail to Survive?

It is fairly easy to account for the abdication of Alfonso. The demise of the monarchy was the result of several years of mounting social crisis. Political and social change had not kept pace with economic change, and Alfonso failed to remedy this. He was finally brought down by the collapse of the Primo de Rivera regime which he himself had installed.

The failure of the Second Republic is more contentious and historians have taken different views as to who was most to blame. One explanation is that the Republic failed because it was systematically undermined by the extreme right wing masquerading as parliamentarians, but an alternative argument is that the left Republic made many avoidable errors, unnecessarily antagonising potential opponents. For example, the Socialists can be accused of irresponsibility in refusing to participate in Popular Front Governments in 1936. Their actions gave the impression that they had abandoned parliamentary methods in favour of revolution and can be considered as a factor in encouraging the right to rebel.

The debate is partly about which side first abandoned legal methods and resorted to violence. The left in the Asturias rising were certainly aiming to seize power by force, but the right had already attempted a coup in the Sanjurjo rising of 1932 and the CEDA's commitment to democracy was always in doubt. Most historians lay the primary responsibility on the Spanish right's determination to use any means to thwart the reasonable reforms of the Republic. For example, George Esenwein and Adrian Shubert assert that 'the Civil War was not the product of any "failure" of the Republic ... what prompted the military rising was not the Republic's failure but quite the opposite: the possibility that it would succeed ... in its programme of wide ranging reform.'[10]

In the confrontational politics of the Second Republic the right, on balance, bears the greater responsibility for the abandonment of legality, though the left also shares some of the blame. What is certain is that provocation on one side was quickly countered by the other in an escalating spiral of violence.

Another way of looking at this issue is to consider whether the Republic was doomed from the start, or whether it would have had a reasonable chance of success had it not been implacably opposed by the right. Sheelagh Ellwood points to the lack of consensus in Spain between 1931 and 1936 about almost everything, including acceptance of a democracy which was anything but firmly established, and the reluctance to abide by the rules of representative government: 'Articulating Parliamentary democracy in Spain between 1931 and 1936 was like attempting to organise a coherent game of football with each team trying to impose its own set of rules, some players squabbling with others on their own side and no-one taking any notice of the referee. Without consensus at least on the minimal objective of implementing democratic rule, confrontation was inevitable.'[11] Certainly Spain had little experience of democracy, and there were groups on both political extremes who were quite ready to resort to violence.

A further problem was that the Republic (unlike the French

Republic), lacked popular support among the middle classes and peasants and it was not in power long enough to improve its standing with these groups. Its strongest backing came from the urban professional and working classes, but these were a minority of the total population. It never commanded the loyalty of either anarchist-influenced labourers increasingly frustrated at the failure of land reform, or of small property holders in areas such as Navarre, who tended to be fiercely Catholic and monarchist.

There was also the European dimension. Though the Civil War stemmed from the Spanish situation, contemporary events in Europe cannot be ignored. The left in Spain was inspired by the example of the Soviet Union, while the right feared Communism. The right drew on the example of Mussolini and Hitler, while the left were determined to avoid the mistakes of their German and Austrian colleagues who had been passive in face of repression.

Faced with the difficulties of modernising a backward economy and social structure in a country without strong democratic traditions, and against the background of the Depression, the Republic was facing insurmountable problems by 1936. Civil War may not have been inevitable but it certainly did not come as a surprise.

References

1   Gerald Brenan, *The Spanish Labyrinth* (CUP, 1943), p.52.
2   Hugh Thomas, *The Spanish Civil War* (Penguin 1986), p.17.
3   Quoted in Raymond Carr, *Spain 1808-1975* (Clarenden, 1982), p.524.
4   Quoted in Thomas, *The Spanish Civil War*, p.29.
5   Henry Buckley, *Life and death of the Spanish Republic* (Hamish Hamilton, 1940) pp. 38-42.
6   Quoted in Paul Preston, *A concise history of the Spanish Civil War* (Fontana Press, 1996), pp.41, 43.
7   Sheelagh Ellwood, *The Spanish Civil War* (Basil Blackwell, 1991), p.18.
8   Leah Manning, *What I saw in Spain* (Gollancz, 1935), pp. 89-112.
9   Alfred Mendizabal, *The martyrdom of Spain* (Geoffrey Bles, 1938), pp.207-211.
10 George Esenwein and Adrian Shubert, *Spain at War* (Longman, 1995), pp. 33-34.
11 Ellwood, *Spanish Civil War*, p.112.

Summary Diagram
Spain from 1898 to 1936

1898 - 1923

Economic and social problems
Dominance of property owners, Church and Army.
Land: latifundia; peasant poverty
Industry: worker/employer conflicts
Growth of Socialism and anarchism

Imperial problems
Loss of colonies 1898
Defeat in Morocco 1921

Political problems
No real democracy.
Political parties unrepresentative.
Disillusionment with the system

The dictatorship of Primo de Rivera 1923-1930

Achievements
Public works and modernisation
Conciliated Socialists
Won Moroccan War
Some prosperity

Problems
Censorship and repression
Economic effects of depression
Opposition from interest groups
Growth of Republicanism

Resignation of Primo January 1930

Fall of the Monarchy April 1931

The Second Republic 1931-1936

The Left Republic 1931-1933
New constitution; Church reform; Army reform; Land reform

Dissatisfaction:
Peasant and workers unrest: CNT risings
Sanjurjo rising 1932
Formation of the CEDA 1933

The Right Republic 1933 -1936
Reforms reversed
Asturias rising October 1933
Popular Front formed November 1935

Cortes elections November 1933

Popular Front Government February - July 1936
Land occupations, strikes and church burnings
Polarisation of right and left
Military coup planned
July 1936: political assassinations

Cortes elections Feb 1936

The Rising 17 July 1936: Civil War starts

Answering source-based questions

Source-based questions can be more easily answered if they are grouped into a few main categories which can be recognised as they appear. The number of marks awarded is usually a guide to how much to write. The main types of questions are:

a) Those (often the first on the paper), which ask you to identify or explain the meaning of a word or phrase. They often require only a short answer.

b) Comprehension questions which ask you to extract information from the source(s) or to show that you have understood a passage by paraphrasing it or expressing it in your own words.

c) Questions which require a comparison of two or more sources, perhaps offering different views of the same event(s).

d) Questions which require you to detect bias in sources.

e) Questions which ask you to analyse the sources, for example to explain how far they support a particular viewpoint or how they explain action and motives.

f) Questions which ask you about the reliability or usefulness to the historian of the evidence in sources. These questions can appear difficult because they are more about the characteristics and nature of the sources than their contents. The following checklist makes it easier to tackle this type of question:

(i) What is the nature of the source? A speech, an official document, memorandum or report, newspaper article, memoirs, extracts from a diary, minutes of a meeting, notes of a conversation, a statistical table?

(ii) Who is writing (or speaking)? Do they have first-hand, or otherwise accurate, knowledge of the event(s)? Is the author impartial or does he/she have an axe to grind?

(iii) When were the source(s) written? At the time or some years after the event? Accounts written many years after the event, such as memoirs, may be unreliable since some facts may have been forgotten or deliberately left out and the writer is often attempting to put himself/herself in a good light and possibly discredit others. For example, a former Nazi writing after the war may produce a selective or distorted account of events in Germany before 1945.

(iv) What is the author's purpose? Are they trying to persuade an audience, as in a speech or a newspaper article, or trying to convince someone in a superior position of their point of view?

(v) If there is more than one source, do they corroborate one another? And if not, why not? Do they accord with your own knowledge of events?

g) Lastly there are questions which ask you to use your own knowledge in addition to extracting material from the sources. These usually require a substantial and detailed answer.

1 Conflicting views on the Asturias Rising

With the points outlined above in mind, read the two sources on pages 20 and 21 on the Asturias Rising, which give two opposing contemporary views of the rising, and answer the following questions. Notice that in the first extract the writer presents Largo Caballero in a favourable light, while portraying the CEDA as fascist. On the other hand, the second extract takes the view that the Socialists readily turned to violence when they could not achieve their aims by parliamentary means, and makes no mention of any fascist characteristics of the CEDA.

a) Identify 'the assault guards' (line 23) and the 'foreign legion' (line 23). (2 marks)

b) Using the extracts and also your own knowledge, explain why the Socialists were determined to resist the entry of the CEDA into the Government. (4 marks)

c) In what ways do the extracts differ in their assessment of Largo Caballero and his policies? (4 marks)

d) On what points do the extracts agree in their descriptions of the rising? (4 marks)

e) In what ways, in their descriptions of the rising, do the two authors reveal their political bias? (6 marks)

f) The first account is based on a visit to Spain a few weeks after the rising, while the second is an eyewitness account of events in Oviedo. Bearing this in mind, what reservations would historians have about using these two sources as evidence of the events of the rising? (5 marks)

3 The Conspiracy and Rising, February to August 1936

1 The Conspiracy and the Conspirators

By the Spring of 1936 the plot to overthrow the government was already taking shape. After the February elections the right had concluded that the Popular Front could not easily be removed except by force - and there were plenty of precedents for coups in Spanish history.

The main impetus for the rebellion came from the army, though political groups were also involved. The main conspirators were a group of senior army officers, including Generals Mola, Goded, Fanjul and Franco, though the latter did not finally decide to join the rebellion until the last moment. Sanjurjo was the nominal leader but, since he had been exiled to Portugal after his failed coup in 1932, Mola became the main organiser, responsible for keeping in touch with fellow conspirators in the army divisions throughout Spain. The plot included a minority of the senior officers but a much higher proportion of the younger, more junior officers, substantiating Azaña's comment that 'Generals under 60 are a national danger.'[1] In 1933 anti-Republican officers had formed the Unión Militar Española, which was estimated to comprise about half those on active service in the middle and lower ranks. Most officers deplored the shift to the left under the Republic, though not all were prepared to hazard the risks of rebellion against a legitimate government. Those in the plot expected to be able to carry the men in their regiments with them. The conspirators had no effective contacts outside Spain, so that the rising was an entirely Spanish enterprise.

There were persistent rumours of a conspiracy during the Spring and Summer of 1936, but the Popular Front governments reacted with surprising nonchalance. The only precaution they took was to transfer some generals to less central or less important commands. Franco was sent to the Canary Islands, Goded to the Balearics and Mola to Pamplona in Navarre in northern Spain. However, this did not greatly impede the conspiracy and, in the case of Mola, placed him in a better position to negotiate with the Carlists.

Before leaving for their new posts, Mola, Goded, Franco and several others met on 8 March at the house of a financier supporter in Madrid, and made a general commitment to rise against the government. It was decided that rebellions would take place in all major towns, Madrid being a major objective. At this stage the rising was only to be put into effect if Largo Caballero, the Socialist leader, took over the government or if a Communist revolution broke out.

There was little consensus among the plotters as to what type of regime would replace the Popular Front government. Mola's aims were expressed in rather vague terms as the establishment of 'order, peace, justice.'[2] Many generals wanted a restoration of the monarchy under Alfonso, but others were not averse to a continuation of the Republic with a suitable 'right-wing' content. Most would probably have been satisfied with any right-wing regime which respected the position of the army. But the Carlists and the Falange, whose participation was important to ensure success, had their own very different opinions as to the future form of government.

The conspirators could depend on some assistance from Alfonsist monarchists, now mainly led by Calvo Sotelo's National Bloc. Gil Robles also supported the embryonic plot and subscribed a large part of the CEDA funds towards it, but the CEDA as an organisation had declined after its electoral defeat in February 1936. More important from a military point of view were the Carlists, who had considerable peasant support in Navarre and possessed in the red-bereted *requetés* a para-military organisation with an estimated 6,000 armed members by 1936.

Mola began negotiations with one of the Carlist leaders, Fal Conde, in the Spring of 1936 but these did not go smoothly due to the latter's insistence on the use of the Carlist flag and Mola's unwillingness to agree to a Carlist restoration. Agreement was not reached until July when the other, more flexible Carlist leader, Rodezno, persuaded Don Carlos' nominee in St. Jean de Luz, across the French border, to support the rising. However, when the rebellion started, it was uncertain what, if anything, the Carlists would gain from it.

On 25 May Mola finally issued a detailed plan for risings in the provinces to be followed by a co-ordinated attack on Madrid, in the event that the city did not immediately fall to the rebels. But the exact timing was determined by a series of political assassinations. On 12 July Falangist gunmen killed a left-wing Assault Guards officer, Castillo. The following day, in reprisal, Calvo Sotelo, a leading monarchist, was kidnapped and shot. Calvo Sotelo was a prominent right-wing member of the Cortes, noted for his aggressive speeches attacking the Popular Front government. His assassination persuaded many who were still vacillating that the government should be overthrown, and it proved to be the signal for the rising.

2 The Falange

Mola had also enlisted the support of the Falange, the Spanish fascist party. Fascism had not gained much ground in Spain by 1936. In contrast with Italy, no fascist movement had emerged in the years immediately following the First World War. Spain was not involved in the war and therefore did not encounter the foreign policy and demobilisation problems experienced in Italy; and the social and economic crisis of the 1920s was, in the short run, relatively successfully resolved by the Primo de Rivera dictatorship. There were, in any case, alternative channels in Spain for right-wing opinion, centring on the CEDA, Catholicism and Carlism, and therefore 'out and out fascism seemed to have little to offer.'[3]

A Spanish fascist party had only emerged in 1931 when the National Syndicalist Offensive (the JONS, after its Spanish initials) was formed by two students, Ledesma Ramos and Redondo y Ortega. Their programme combined nationalism and anti-parliamentarianism with radical ideas. In October 1933, another fascist party, the Falange Española, more upper-class in composition but with similar views, was founded by José Antonio Primo de Rivera, the son of the former dictator. In 1934 the two groups merged under the general name of the Falange, with a uniformed para-military body, the blueshirts.

José Antonio was a charismatic young aristocrat with revolutionary and romantic ideas, fond of making such pronouncements as 'our place is in the fresh air, under the cloudless heavens, weapons in our hands, with the stars above us.'[4] The Falange policies were similar to those of the Italian fascists. Its programme espoused nationalism and the revival of the Spanish Empire, and advocated strong authoritarian leadership to replace parliament, democracy and political parties. José Antonio equally despised parties of both the left and the right and described the fascist movement as 'anti-party'. The Falange was against socialism and communism, but its programme of November 1934 committed it to radical social change, to be achieved in the framework of a totalitarian state, as shown in the following extract:

1 We reject the capitalist system which disregards the needs of the people, dehumanises private property and transforms the workers into shapeless masses prone to misery and despair.
   The primary purpose of wealth is to effect an improvement in the
5 standard of living of all the people - it is intolerable that great masses of people live in poverty while a few enjoy luxury.
   All Spanish citizens are entitled to employment. The public institutions will provide for the maintenance of those who are involuntarily out of work.
10 We shall achieve a social organisation of agriculture by redistributing all the arable land so as to promote family holdings.[5]

Yet in spite of these left-seeming policies, the Falange made little headway with the working class, to whom genuine socialism or anarchism had much greater appeal. By the beginning of 1936, it had only about 8,000 members, mostly university students, attracted by the prospect of adventure and excitement. As a Falange member later recalled: 'to concentrate on work was an impossible and reprehensible attitude ... pistols lay behind books.'[6]

The Falange had little success in the February 1936 elections, though it did gain more supporters in the following months, and was boosted by the adherence of the CEDA youth movement (the JAP). Its involvement in street fighting and disorder led to its being disbanded by the government in March 1936 and José Antonio and other leaders were imprisoned. Whilst in prison, José Antonio was in contact with the leaders of the conspiracy, but he had little in common with them, and they in turn had no sympathy with his advocacy of social reform. He was rightly suspicious that the army intended to use the Falange for its own purposes and dispense with it later, and only on 29 June did he finally instruct his followers to join in the rebellion, though at the same time insisting that the Falange retain a distinct identity and separate military units. On 12 July he was warning (correctly as it turned out), against 'the establishment of a false, conservative fascism without revolutionary courage and young blood.'[7]

3 Franco

Though at first hesitant about joining the rising, Franco was quickly to become its leader. Francisco Franco was born in 1892 into a middle-class naval family in Galicia in north-west Spain. Owing to lack of opportunities in the navy following the naval disaster in the Spanish-American War of 1898, he decided instead to join the army, and after training at the military academy in Toledo was posted to Morocco in 1912. Franco took enthusiastically to military life and achieved success and rapid promotion in the Moroccan campaigns, returning to the mainland in 1926 as one of Spain's youngest generals. Meantime he had married Carmen Polo, whom he had met while based in Oviedo, and by 1927 was looking forward to enjoying family life together with a prestigious post as Director of the Military Academy at Saragossa.

Franco had been brought up to be devoutly religious and his military training had strengthened his beliefs in hierarchy and obedience to established authority. He had no time for parliament or democracy and these views were reinforced by his experience of the Republic between 1931 and 1936, especially when it closed the Saragossa military academy. In 1934 his fortunes improved when the right Republican government appointed him as Army Chief of Staff, as a reward for his part in suppressing the Asturias rising, but in March 1936 they declined again when he was demoted to the Governorship of the Canaries.

Franco had few political connections before 1936, except for some contacts with the CEDA, and no involvement with fascism. His political ideas were few, simple and rigid. He felt that government was best run on military lines. He disliked political parties, which he felt had contributed to Spain's decline, and viewed the election of the Popular Front government in 1936 with dismay. But in spite of this he was reluctant at first to support the conspiracy, his coyness causing him to be nicknamed 'Miss Canary Islands' by the other generals. He counselled caution (a characteristic which was to be much in evidence during the civil war), apparently wishing to be on the winning side without taking too many risks. As late as 23 June he wrote an ambivalent letter to the Prime Minister, Casares Quiroga, implying that although the army was hostile to the Republic, he himself might be loyal. Although the aircraft which was to fly him to Morocco was chartered as early as 9 July he did not finally make up his mind to join the rising until after the assassination of Calvo Sotelo.

4 The Rising

The date for the rising was set for 18 July when simultaneous actions by the garrisons in all major cities and towns were to take place. However, due to the premature discovery of the plot in Morocco, the army there was obliged to rise a day early on 17 July, when the Foreign Legion took over Melilla, followed by the other main Moroccan towns. The rebellion then spread to mainland Spain. Risings did not occur on the same day as planned, since the momentum had been disrupted by the timing being brought forward in Morocco. On 18 July there were rebellions in Andalusia, including Seville, but not till 19 July in Madrid, Barcelona, Pamplona and Saragossa. In some places success or failure was not determined till 20 July or later. Meanwhile Franco had arrived in Morocco and taken command there.

In Madrid, news of the rebellion created panic, which the Prime Minister, Casares Quiroga, was unable to quell: 'His Ministry is a madhouse and the maddest inmate is the Prime Minister. He is neither eating nor sleeping. He shouts and screams as if possessed. He will hear nothing of arming the people and threatens to shoot anyone who takes it upon himself to do so.'[8]

A chaotic few hours later Casares resigned, but his successor, Martiñez Barrio, was no more successful. He telephoned Mola in Pamplona on the evening of 18 July to try to negotiate a compromise, which included offering Mola a cabinet position. This Mola refused, and on 19 July Martiñez in turn resigned to make way for a government headed by Giral which finally made a decision to give arms to the various workers' militias (armed groups attached to the political parties), in Madrid so that they might help defend the Republic.

5 The Rising: Success and Failure

While the telephone and, to some extent, radio broadcasts, played a part in co-ordinating the rising - the Civil War was the first important military event of the telephone age - events in Spain's provinces and cities developed quite differently. The rebels triumphed in the conservative regions of Navarre and Castile in northern Spain, in Pamplona, Burgos, Valladolid, Salamanca and Saragossa (though the latter was a centre of anarchist activity), and in parts of Andalusia. But Seville was the only city of any importance to fall to them. The rising had failed in the main centres of industry - Bilbao, Santander, Barcelona and Valencia and, most importantly, in the capital, Madrid (see the map of the division of Spain in July 1936 on page 35).

The success or failure of the rebellion was determined by a variety of factors. The most important was the attitude of the officers of the various garrisons. The army proved in the event to be evenly divided - half supported the rising and half remained loyal to the government. Also important was the attitude of the Civil and Assault Guards. As it happened some of the Civil Guards and most of the Assault Guards opposed the rebellion. The loyalty of the Assault Guards was not surprising since they had been established by the Republic as a left-wing counterweight to the Civil Guard. The fact that significant numbers of Civil Guards, previously noted for their repression of workers and peasants, stuck by the government was more surprising and had not been foreseen by the conspirators.

The attitude of the local population also counted, especially where armed militias or para-military groups were in existence. For example working-class militias contributed to the defeat of the rising in Barcelona and Madrid, though some historians regard their role as secondary to that of the army. Civilian support certainly helped ensure its success in Pamplona, Burgos and other towns in northern Spain. Carlist *requetés* (para-military groups), were important in reinforcing Mola's troops in Navarre, though the Falange blueshirts played a more peripheral role in the rebellion.

Decisive action by individuals was also a factor, as in Seville, where General Queipo de Llano with very few troops bluffed his way to control of a city with a large working-class population. He then proceeded to make a series of bloodthirsty radio broadcasts, threatening Republicans with retribution. In Oviedo in the Asturias, Colonel Aranda, by first pretending to support the government, tricked 4,000 miners into departing for Madrid, leaving him to seize control of the town. On the other hand the vacillation of the officers in Madrid greatly reduced their chances of taking the capital city.

In Pamplona, Mola encountered few problems. This town was the centre of Carlism and the revolt had a genuinely popular basis. In Burgos too the Nationalists were largely supported by the local population and quickly took over. By 19 July troops from Navarre were ready to advance southwards.

In Barcelona, however, the situation was completely different. The city was firmly pro-Republican with a strong anarchist presence. The rebels' plan was for troops from the various military barracks on the outskirts to converge on the city centre. Companys, the President of the Catalan government, the Generalitat, had refused to distribute arms to the workers, but on the evening of 18 July the anarchist union, the CNT, took over several arms depots and called for a general strike. The following morning, after a tense night, soldiers from the barracks in the north of the city began to march towards the

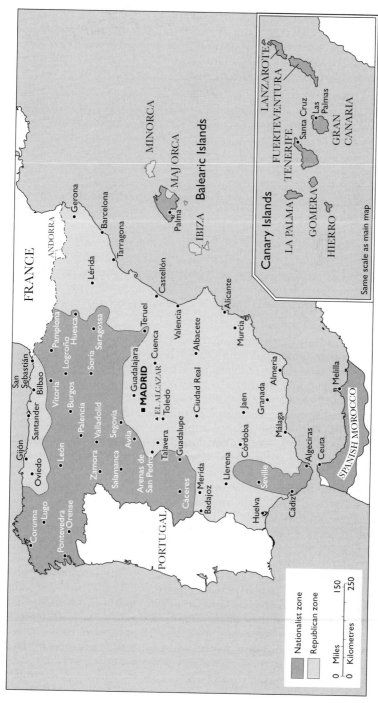

The division of Spain in July 1936

Canary Islands

LANZAROTE

FUERTEVENTURA

TENERIFE

Santa Cruz

Las Palmas

GRAN CANARIA

LA PALMA

GOMERA

HIERRO

Same scale as main map

FRANCE

ANDORRA

Gerona

Barcelona

Tarragona

Lérida

MINORCA

MAJORCA

Palma

IBIZA

Balearic Islands

Castellón

Valencia

Alicante

Teruel

Cuenca

Albacete

Murcia

Almería

Granada

Málaga

Ciudad Real

Toledo

EL ALCAZAR

MADRID

Guadalajara

Segovia

Ávila

Arenas de San Pedro

Talavera

Guadalupe

Mérida

Llerena

Córdoba

Jaen

Seville

Huelva

Cádiz

Algeciras

Ceuta

Melilla

SPANISH MOROCCO

Cáceres

Badajoz

PORTUGAL

Salamanca

Zamora

Valladolid

Palencia

León

Burgos

Soria

Logroño

Vitoria

Pamplona

Huesca

Saragossa

Bilbao

San Sebastián

Santander

Gijón

Oviedo

Lugo

Coruña

Pontevedra

Orense

Nationalist zone

Republican zone

0   Miles   150

0   Kilometres   250

Plaza de Cataluña. But they were unable to join forces with other regiments due to resistance from anarchist militias, Assault Guards and Civil Guards. This eyewitness account by a journalist attributes the failure of the rising in Barcelona to resistance by the Assault Guard, the Civil Guard and the ordinary inhabitants of the city:

> 1 At 5 o'clock [on 19 July] the first shots disturbed Barcelona's uneasy sleep. ... If the troops marching from the north could cross the central square, the Plaza Cataluña, and make the junction with Alarazana at the other end of the Ramblas, the main part of the city would be cut in two
> 5 and the two semi-circles would be reduced by other columns moving round their perimeter, the Rondas. ... The first columns had exchanged shots with a few police patrols who retired before overwhelming odds, but when the troops arrived at the outer circles of the inner city the Calle Cortes ... resistance was intense. At first the action was sustained
> 10 by the shock police and loyal civil guards supported by a few militia patrols but soon the whole population of Barcelona joined in. ... The battle began furiously ... The militia, men, women and children fought like furies ... It was now perfectly clear that this was an officers' putsch ... the soldiers realising how they had been deceived, fraternised with
> 15 the workers wherever they could. ... The insurrection was lost as soon as the soldiers fraternised and the militia had arms.[9]

Fighting continued for most of the day. Some troops succeeded in occupying the telephone building but were quickly dislodged. The rebels' problems were compounded by the fact that Goded, the general in charge of the Barcelona rising, only arrived from Majorca on the morning of the 19th some hours after the start of the rebellion. He set up his headquarters in the Capitancy General near the harbour, but this building was stormed and Goded was captured. By Monday 20 July the rising in Barcelona had been decisively defeated.

Events in Madrid did not get under way until 19/20 July. One quarter of the officers on active service were stationed there but by no means all supported the conspiracy. Effective planning was lacking and, at first, there was some confusion as to who would command the rising in the capital. On 19 July General Fanjul emerged as the leader but he lingered till too late in the Montana barracks on the outskirts of the city. Some insurgent troops did attempt to advance into the centre, but were driven back, partly by the Socialist UGT and the CNT militias, which by then had obtained arms. The Civil Guards were also largely loyal. The photograph on page 37 depicts the solidarity between the workers and the Civil Guards in Madrid - note the distinctive uniform and hat worn by the Civil Guard.

On 20 July the Montana barracks, where the rebels were holding out, were finally stormed and captured. This account by a foreign journalist based in Madrid emphasises the part played by the militias in defeating the rising:

1 The Government on 18 July gave an order to arm the people. Minutes
later police wagons loaded with heavy boxes were racing through the
streets to the trade union and political HQs where anxious crowds
stood wondering whether they were to survive or be crushed. In
5 Madrid the officers simply could not make up their minds to take the
plunge ... A soldier whom I knew described to me afterwards how the
officers in their quarters argued furiously hour after hour as to whether
they should rebel or not. General Fanjul waited till Monday morning [20
July] before he showed signs of rebellion. On Monday morning I awoke
10 to hear the boom of cannon ... Out on the streets I saw a new Madrid.
Overnight the youths, girls and more mature citizens of the trade
unions and political organisations had adopted a more or less general
uniform of a blue overall. Cars had been requisitioned. Groups of
workers drove fast and furiously around the town having the time of
15 their lives ... A picturesque but determined motley of police, soldiers,
workers, lookers-on, assaulted the Montana barracks furiously with the
aid of some ancient artillery and some light bombs dropped from aeroplanes. In four or five hours the battle was over. The mob rushed the
gate. About 160 fascists who were caught were shot in the courtyard.[10]

Madrid was saved but the rebels had prevailed elsewhere, and by 20
July it was clear that the rising had left Spain divided between the

Civil guards and militiamen

Republican Government and its opponents, who began to describe themselves, and be described as, Nationalists.

6 The First Stages of the War, July to August 1936

In July 1936 the Nationalists controlled rather less than half of Spain (see the map on page 35) To improve their position it was essential for them to deploy the 24,000 experienced troops of the Army of Africa, including the Foreign Legion and Moors. These might tip the balance, but only provided they could be transported to mainland Spain across the Straits of Gibraltar. The airlift of these troops, a result of German and Italian aid, was undoubtedly the most important development of the first weeks of the war. 1,500 troops were transported by the beginning of August and 3,000 ferried in a convoy of merchant ships with Italian bomber cover on 5 August. From 6 August, 500 were airlifted each day.

On 6 August Franco arrived in Seville and the Army of Africa set off northwards commanded by Colonel Yagüe, an *africanista*. Having covered 300 miles in a month, it reached Talavera de Reina which was within striking distance of Madrid. Along the way the province of Extremadura and the towns of Merida and Badajoz were captured, accompanied by a systematic policy of terror and the killing of thousands of Republicans. The Republican militias tried to stem the advance but were ineffective against the experienced Moroccan Legionnaires and were not aided by regular Republican troops.

Meanwhile, Nationalist troops under Mola set off from Pamplona, Burgos and Valladolid to advance on Madrid from the north, but were temporarily halted in the Guadarrama mountain range by a combination of militia opposition and a shortage of arms and ammunition. Mola's forces did, however, take Irún and San Sebastian on the frontier in early September 1936, an important victory which cut the Basque communications with France.

The first six weeks of the war were crucial in giving the Nationalists, after a shaky start, a much stronger base from which they could not easily be dislodged. By early September they had made significant gains, having conquered all the territory along the Portuguese frontier and extended and consolidated their hold on Andalusia. Franco certainly benefited from prompt German and Italian aid, but this does not entirely explain the greater Nationalist success. The Republic failed to take the initiative in the early stages of the war and its tactics were largely defensive. This lost it valuable time. More decisive action, possibly utilising its (admittedly small) airforce and navy, might have impeded the transport of the army of Africa to southern Spain - though the navy was weakened by lack of officers and was denied by Britain the use of the refuelling facilities in Gibraltar. Equally, a determined advance southwards might have consolidated the Republican positions in Andalusia, while an advance south-westwards, from Madrid to the Portuguese frontier, could have prevented Franco's troops from joining forces with Mola. The Republic did send a force to try to recapture Córdoba, but with no success.

As it was, Franco and Mola were able to join forces in preparation for an onslaught on Madrid. The Republic still held the capital city but apart from this had few achievements to its credit apart from crushing the remnants of nationalist resistance in Valencia and Albacete, capturing the barracks in Gijón in the Asturias, and briefly occupying the island of Ibiza. The Nationalists, however, were still holding out in Oviedo in the Asturias and in the Alcázar (fortress) in Toledo.

7 Republican and Nationalist Spain in August 1936

By the end of August, although the two sides were roughly equal in geographical area, the Republic still had some significant advantages. It controlled most of the major cities and all the main industrial areas including Catalonia, the Basque country and the Asturias (though the latter was separated from the rest of the Republic by a swathe of Nationalist territory). It therefore possessed the heavy industry vital for the production of armaments, although it would be difficult to fully utilise these resources without imports of raw materials. Since the Republic held the gold reserves, it also had the wherewithal to purchase arms from abroad. Also in Republican territory at the beginning of the war were the regions producing the main agricultural exports, citrus fruits and olive oil - though these were to be captured by the Nationalists by 1937. Control of Madrid, with the apparatus of government, was a considerable practical and psychological advantage. And the Republic was, after all, the legitimate, elected government, entitled to be recognised as such by foreign states, as opposed to the Nationalists, who only had the status of rebels.

The Nationalists, on the other hand, had acquired most of the food producing areas. They were supported by Portugal, where the Salazar dictatorship was highly sympathetic and facilitated communication along the frontier between their zones. Their greatest advantage was immediate aid, from late July onwards, from Germany and Italy in the form of transport and fighter aircraft, whereas the Republic received little foreign assistance till October.

Both sides faced political problems in the Summer of 1936. In the Republic there were differences between Socialists, anarchists and Communists. And in the Nationalist camp too, the different groups involved in the rebellion had few common aims except for the overthrow of the Popular Front government.

The loyalties of the civilian population were sometimes arbitrarily determined by the location Spaniards found themselves in when the war began. But, in general, the majority of the upper and wealthier middle classes, including many senior civil servants, supported the Nationalists, while most of the working class supported the Republic. The middle classes were more evenly divided, their allegiance depending on their financial or occupational status or their political views. The peasants were also divided. While the landless labourers of the south were pro-Republic, substantial numbers of peasants in north and central Spain preferred the Nationalist cause out of fear for property rights or out of religious belief. The Catalans and Basques supported the Republic which had granted them autonomy.

The main weakness of the Republic lay in its armed forces. The Spanish army had evenly divided, with seventy-five per cent of generals supporting the Republic and two-thirds of officers lower down in rank supporting the rebellion. It has been estimated that about sixty per cent of the Civil Guard and the Assault Guard remained loyal as did most of the air force and navy. On many ships the men had mutinied against their pro-Nationalist officers. However, while the Nationalist part of the army simply continued to function as usual, the Republican army was in disarray. One problem was that Republican politicians did not trust the loyalty of the remaining officers, a suspicion sometimes, though not always, justified. Another was the existence of the militias, which were a law unto themselves and conflicted with the regular army. Hence the CNT militias from Barcelona decided in July to concentrate on recapturing Saragossa, which was a centre of anarchist activity but not strategically important, when they would have been better deployed in campaigns in southern and western Spain. Militias were highly committed and full of revolutionary enthusiasm but this did not make up for their lack of military training.

Therefore, while the immediate results of the coup had been disappointing for the Nationalists, by the end of August 1936 they had made some significant territorial gains and the opposing forces were more evenly balanced. This, combined with foreign aid, was to turn an audacious coup into a prolonged civil war.

References

1   Raymond Carr, *The Spanish Tragedy* (Weidenfeld & Nicolson, 1977), p.67.
2   Hugh Thomas, *The Spanish Civil War* (Penguin, 1986) p.173.
3   Martin Blinkhorn (ed), *Fascists and Conservatives; the radical right and the establishment in twentieth century Europe* (Unwin Hyman, 1990), p.130.
4   F.L. Carsten, *The rise of Fascism* (Batsford, 1982), p.198.
5   Quoted in Harry Browne, *Spain's Civil War* (Longman, 1996), pp.112-13.
6   Raymond Carr, *Spain 1808-1975* (Clarendon, 1981), p.648.
7   Carsten, *The rise of Fascism*, p.201.
8   Carr, *The Spanish Tragedy*, p.72.
9   F. Jellenek, *The Civil War in Spain* (1938), pp.268-324.
10 Henry Buckley, *The life and death of the Spanish Republic* (Hamish Hamilton, 1940), pp.38-42.

Summary Diagram
The Conspiracy and Rising, February to August 1936

The Conspiracy and Conspirators

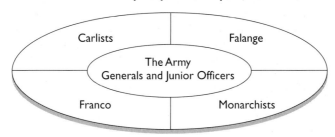

Carlists

Falange

The Army
Generals and Junior Officers

Franco

Monarchists

The Rising 17 - 20 July 1936

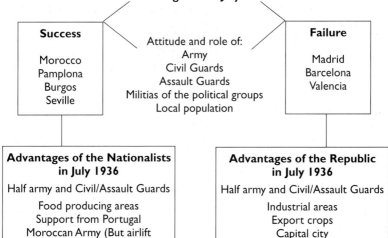

Success

Morocco
Pamplona
Burgos
Seville

Attitude and role of:
Army
Civil Guards
Assault Guards
Militias of the political groups
Local population

Failure

Madrid
Barcelona
Valencia

Advantages of the Nationalists in July 1936

Half army and Civil/Assault Guards

Food producing areas
Support from Portugal
Moroccan Army (But airlift necessary)

Advantages of the Republic in July 1936

Half army and Civil/Assault Guards

Industrial areas
Export crops
Capital city
Gold reserve
Legitimate government

Republican problems in July 1936
Unreliability of Army
Militias
No co-ordinated military strategy

Nationalist gains by end of August 1936
Airlift of Army of Morocco to southern Spain
Franco's advance northwards to within striking distance of Madrid
Hold on Andulasia consolidated
Irún on French frontier captured

Answering essay questions on the causes of the Civil War

To answer questions on the origins of the Civil War you need a knowledge both of the material in Chapter 2 and some of the material (on the conspiracy) in this chapter. Essay questions generally focus on the period from 1919 to July 1936, and especially on the Second Republic, but they may also require discussion of longer-term factors, going back to the period before the First World War. Some questions deal with the failure of the monarchy as well as that of the Republic.

Examples of essay questions are :
1. Why did neither monarchy nor democracy survive in Spain between 1919 and 1939?
2. Why, after 1919, were both monarchy and democracy successively overthrown in Spain ?
3. When and why did it begin to seem that civil war in Spain could not be avoided?
4. 'It was the intransigence of the left rather than the strengths of the right that caused the Spanish Civil War.' Discuss.

There may also be questions specifically on Primo de Rivera's regime, for example:
5. How far do you agree that while Primo de Rivera brought political stability to Spain, he did nothing to resolve the deep divisions in Spanish society?

Most of these questions are asking for a list of reasons to explain 'why' certain events happened. Too much narrative should be avoided. For example in answering question 1, you should make separate lists of reasons to explain the failure of both the monarchy and of the Republic. Some reasons may be common to both. You would have to determine how much weight to give to the different parts of the question, and an appropriate ratio would be to spend one-third of the time on the monarchy and two-thirds on the Republic. A typical list of reasons for the fall of the monarchy might include:
a) Political problems: e.g. no real democracy and a shallow basis of support for the political system and parties.
b) Economic and social problems: e.g. a socially divided society; industrial and agrarian problems; the impact of the socialists and anarchists.
c) Imperial problems, culminating in the defeats in Morocco, which brought about the Primo de Rivera regime.
d) The failure of Primo by 1929 and the implications of this for the monarchy
e) The events of 1930-31; the municipal elections of April 1931 and Alfonso's abdication.

The failure of the Republic would require analysis of the responsibility of both left and right. A list of reasons should include:
a) Problems of church reform
b) Problems of land reform

c) Problems of army reform
d) Opposition from the left
e) Opposition from the right; the CEDA
f) Increasing political polarisation from 1933-5; the Asturias rising
g) Events under the Popular Front government in 1936
h) The conspiracy to overthrow the Republic
i) Ending with a brief description of the rising in July 1936

Having compiled a list of points in your plan you would then have to weigh the importance of each factor. For example in the question above you might decide that the religious and agrarian reforms of the Republic roused more widespread opposition than army reform. The attitude and role of the CEDA are important in helping polarise political opinion in Spain, as is the Asturias rising.

Questions based on quotations often appear more difficult than they really are and it is important to realise that there is not necessarily any right or wrong answer. The examiners are looking for analysis backed up by evidence, and you must provide factual evidence for any argument you put forward. For example in question 4 you should separately examine the role of the left and right in Spain between 1931 and 1936 and then reach some conclusions. You may decide that the left contributed to the outbreak of the civil war by making several disastrous mistakes and miscalculations, but that the right was mainly to blame since it was determined to use extra-parliamentary methods to prevent reasonable reforms and finally resorted to armed rebellion.

The section on the left should include the following points:

a) Church and land reforms of the Republic which possibly unnecessarily antagonised Catholics and property owners.
b) Anarchist risings and disturbances between 1931 and 1934.
c) The Asturias rising in 1934 which had the effect of persuading the Socialists under Largo Caballero to move further to the left and advocate revolution.
d) The refusal of the Socialists to participate in the 1936 Popular Front Government.
e) The wave of strikes, land occupations and church burnings in Spring and Summer 1936 which substantiated the impression that Spain was on the verge of revolution.

The section on the right would include:

a) The determination of the right not to accept the Republic and to oppose reform.
b) An evaluation of the strength of the CEDA and of its policies, which seemed to border on fascism, by the end of 1934.
c) An evaluation of the strength of the Falange and other right-wing groups, including Alfonsist and Carlist monarchists, by 1936.
d) The army conspiracy in 1936 to overthrow the Republic; how much support did this attract? Did the anti-Republicans deliberately exaggerate the threat of revolution in 1936?

4 Republican Spain from July 1936 to March 1939

Throughout the Civil War, the Republic was beset by internal problems and crises. During the first few weeks of the war there were three changes of government as successive prime ministers grappled unsuccessfully with the problems of the rising. In September 1936 Largo Caballero, the Socialist leader, became Prime Minister, but his regime was undermined by conflict between rival political groups and in May 1937 he was replaced by Juan Negrín. Negrín's government survived till the end of the war but with the corollary of much greater Communist and Soviet influence.

One difficulty faced by the Republic was that the parties which supported it subscribed to a wide variety of incompatible ideologies, ranging from moderate Republicans to anarchists and non-communist Marxists. Another was that during the rising the Madrid government had lost control to workers' anti-fascist committees, which sprang up spontaneously all over the Republican zone. Power shifted to the left and also downwards to the regions, as Catalonia, Aragon, the Basque region and the Asturias became virtually independent of the central government. These developments led the communist politician Dolores Ibárruri to assert that 'the whole state apparatus was destroyed and state power lay in the streets.'[1] Though an exaggeration, this statement illustrates the disorganised state of the Republic at the start of the war.

These problems were never wholly resolved and an important question to consider when reading this chapter is how far they weakened the Republic and contributed to its defeat. An associated issue is whether the eventual Communist domination was beneficial or disadvantageous to the Republic and to its efforts to win the war.

1 Governments and Revolution in the Summer of 1936

Ironically the rising precipitated the very revolution it had sought to prevent. In the power vacuum it created, middle-of-the-road Republicans and moderate Socialists were displaced by anarchists and revolutionary Socialists, who took over the functions of government, forming militias and running industry and transport. The anarchists, as the largest left-wing group in Spain at the time, were in a strong position in Catalonia, Aragon and Andalusia, while in Madrid and Valencia left-wing Socialists played the main role.

In September 1936, Giral, the moderate Republican leader, was replaced by the Socialist Largo Caballero, who formed a government of Socialists, Communists and liberals. On 4 November 1936, against their political instincts, four anarchists were induced to join. This involved the anarchist leadership in government decision-making which was later to make it easier to divide them and to suppress the anarchist-promoted revolution. There were thus considerable differences of opinion within the government, and the Socialist Party was also divided, since Largo, popularly known as the 'Spanish Lenin', had become distinctly more left-wing than his colleague and rival, Prieto.

In Catalonia, the government also moved to the left. After the defeat of the rising in Barcelona, Companys, the President of the Generalitat, had been obliged to share power with an Anti-Fascist Militia Committee dominated by the anarchists. At the end of September when this committee dissolved itself, the CNT, the PSUC (the Catalan combined Communist and Socialist party) and the POUM joined the Esquerra (the moderate Republican Party) on the Generalitat. The POUM was a small, recently established, Catalan-based party, categorised by its opponents as Trotskyist - its leader, Nin, had at one time been Trotsky's secretary. However, it did not subscribe to all of Trotsky's views and is best described as a Marxist party which was critical of the Soviet system and particularly of Stalin's policies. It was therefore very unpopular with the Communists.

In Aragon a defence council was established by the anarchist leader, Ascaso, and for the first year of the war this region operated as an independent state. Meantime, separate governments were also set up in the Basque region and the Asturias.

The workers' committees quickly seized the chance to put revolutionary theories into practice. The resulting social and economic transformation was the culmination of pressure for change which had been building up since 1931, and particularly since February 1936. The effects, however, were far more radical than anything envisaged under the Second Republic. The rising offered an unprecedented opportunity to eliminate the power of upper and middle class, and to replace it with control by workers and peasants. The Church was a particular object of hostility, and many churches were burnt and clergy driven out, imprisoned or killed. Revolution was most in evidence in Barcelona, where the Ritz hotel was turned into a workers' canteen and where anyone wearing a hat or a tie, symbols of middle-class dress, was regarded with suspicion. The euphoric atmosphere in the city is vividly described in this extract by the writer George Orwell, who fought for the Republic in a POUM militia:

1   It was the first time that I had ever been in a town where the working
    class was in the saddle. Practically every building of any size had been
    seized by the workers and was draped with ... the red and black flag
    of the Anarchists; every wall was scrawled with the hammer and sickle
5   and with the initials of the revolutionary parties; almost every church
    had been gutted and its images burnt. Churches here and there were
    being systematically demolished by gangs of workmen. Every shop and

café had an inscription saying that it had been collectivised; even the
bootblacks had been collectivised and their boxes painted red and
10 black. Waiters and shop-walkers looked you in the face and treated you
as an equal ... Tipping was forbidden by law ... There were no private
motor-cars, they had all been commandeered ... Down the Ramblas,
the wide central artery of the town where crowds of people streamed
15 constantly to and fro, the loudspeakers were bellowing revolutionary
songs all day and far into the night ... Practically everyone wore rough
working-class clothes, or blue overalls, or some variant of the militia
uniform ... There was much [in this] that I did not understand, in some
ways I did not even like it, but I recognised it immediately as a state of
20 affairs worth fighting for.[2]

2 Collectivisation in Industry and Agriculture

The most important change brought about by the summer revolution
was the establishment of collectives in industry and agriculture,
owned and controlled by the workforce. This adventurous social
experiment derived mainly from anarchist ideas, though collectives
were also set up by the POUM and left Socialists.

In all, about 2,000 factories and retail businesses were collectivised
and about 2,500 agricultural collectives set up. Collectivisation thus
involved more than 1.5 million people. It was most extensive in
Catalonia, Aragon and those parts of Andalusia not conquered by the
Nationalists. Madrid, Valencia and the north were less affected. By
October 1936, 70 percent of all enterprises in Barcelona had been
collectivised including transport and public utilities, such as elec-
tricity, compared with 30 per cent in Madrid, where collectivisation
was mainly confined to the war industries.

a) Collectivisation of industry

This took a variety of forms. In some firms private ownership was
allowed to continue, with union control over decision making. In
most cases, however, the owners were expropriated (many having fled
or been imprisoned), and the firms were declared owned by the workforce and run by a committee elected by the workers, or by the trade
unions. Some industries, for example timber, were 'socialised', which
meant that all the stages of production were integrated and run by
one committee.

Government attitudes to collectivisation were at best ambivalent,
and more usually hostile, though in Catalonia, where most large and
medium size enterprises were collectivised, the Generalitat legalised
those with over 100 workers, exempting only small and foreign-owned
enterprises.

Collectivisation was popular with most workers. Piece work

payments, disliked as divisive, since they depended on the amount produced and set workers in competition with one another, were abolished in favour of hourly pay rates. On the other hand, working hours often increased, especially in war production industries. The main advantage of collectives was the opportunity to have more say in decision-making, as described by this textile worker:

> 1 He noticed one big difference in the workforce after collectivisation. Prior to the war, none of the workers 'knew how to talk'. ... But the moment the factory was collectivised and there were general assemblies everyone started to talk ... They obviously felt themselves in
> 5 charge now and with the right to speak for themselves.[3]

But while the collectives offered workers an opportunity for greater control over their working lives, they soon ran into economic difficulties. Textiles, the main Catalan industry, faced shortages of imported raw cotton due to the Nationalist naval blockade, and when existing stocks ran out the factories were reduced to a two or three day week. Coal was in short supply, since the Asturias, from which most of it came, was cut off from the rest of the Republic and, by 1937, conquered by the Nationalists. Consumer industries could not sell their goods in the smaller and contracting home market. Nor was it easy to convert industry to armaments production, though there were some ingenious schemes, such as transforming lip-stick case manufacture into the production of cartridges. In addition, the banks had not been collectivised and so were unwilling to make loans to the collectivised industries, forcing them to become dependent on the government for support.

The most serious failing of the collectives was their inability to meet the demands of a war economy. The difficulties of negotiating with independent collectives are described in this account by a government official of his efforts to procure lorries from the Barcelona motor industry:

> 1 At the end of October 1936 I went to the General Motors plant in Barcelona and the factory committee met to consider my request. I explained to them that as the railway communications with Madrid were practically cut, we were forced to provision Madrid by road and
> 5 that we therefore needed lorries. The committee gave me a sympathetic hearing...
>
> 'Don't worry comrade ... the comrade who has just left has gone to summon the foremen of the various workshops to arrange shifts for mounting the chassis as soon as possible. We shan't stop working till
> 10 every single one of them is properly fitted up and ready to go to Madrid.'
>
> I returned to General motors next day.
>
> 'Part of the work is finished and we have turned out thirty lorries already, but we have some very unpleasant news for you ... Vallejo has

15 forbidden the chassis to be mounted and said they must not be sent to
   Madrid.'
      'Who is Vallejo?'
      'He is the secretary of the Barcelona War Industries committee…'
20   I found Vallejo seated at a desk full of telephones which were
   constantly ringing. He sat there giving innumerable orders as though he
   were a chief of staff … 'You want us to put the industries of Catalonia
   at the disposal of Madrid,' he said, 'and now you want to take our lorries.
   But the Government refuses to grant us foreign exchange which
25 prevents us from buying raw materials and coal and condemns our
   industries to unemployment. You people in Madrid are idiotic enough to
   order your army uniforms from the rickety industries of Valencia simply
   because you are frightened of the revolution and don't want to come to
   terms with us…'
30   That night when I faced the committee I found them all waiting for
   me with their claws out … I explained that if Madrid fell, Catalonia
   would be quite unable to complete its brilliant revolution for the simple
   reason that it would not be allowed time … Two days later a hundred
   lorries had reached Valencia. [4]

Though the official eventually succeeded in his quest, note the
considerable power wielded by the collective leader and also the
extent to which regional rivalries were hindering the war effort.

Catalan industry was vital to the Republic, the more so since the
other industrial areas in northern Spain soon fell to Franco. The
Madrid and Catalan governments tried to control the collectives but
to little avail, so that in the end there was no alternative but to restore
private enterprise or, more usually, introduce direct state control.

b) Collectivisation of agriculture

In the Summer and Autumn of 1936 about 2,500 agrarian collectives
were set up covering 9 million acres, the process going furthest in
Aragon and in Andalusia.

The establishment of such a collective was typically preceded by the
arrival of an anarchist militia column which would burn the church,
drive out any known right-wingers and call an assembly to discuss
collectivising the land (a process depicted in a lively scene in the film
'Land and Freedom'). When the principle of collectivisation had
been agreed, as it almost always was, a committee would be set up,
usually answerable in theory to a general assembly of all the peasants.
All land and equipment would henceforth be commonly owned, to be
worked by the peasants in family or neighbourhood groups, the
produce going into a common pool controlled by the committee. In
theory, food and other commodities were to be distributed according
to need, but in practice this soon broke down to be replaced by
rationing on the basis of an individual or family 'wage'. A distinctive

feature of collectives was the abolition of money and its replacement by vouchers which could be exchanged for food and other necessities.

In Andalusia where anarchism was strongly based, the rural population of landless labourers was easily persuaded of the merits of collectives. In Aragon, on the other hand, the small and medium peasants were more reluctant to give up their individual holdings. It is difficult to determine to what extent peasants were forced into collectives - sometimes they might be allowed to retain individual plots of land, though in this case they might face hostility from the collectivised peasants. Many small peasants opposed the changes, though the collectives were not necessarily as unpopular as was claimed by their opponents. Work on the collectivised land might be hard and standards of living low, but then most small proprietors had been poor prior to collectivisation and any further deterioration could be blamed on the hardships of war. As in industry collectives provided more opportunities for participation in decision making, though in some cases peasants might be exchanging landowner control for committee control. There were, however, wide discrepancies between rich and poor collectives which contradicted the egalitarian principles on which they were based. A balanced view is given in these recollections of a member of an Aragon collective:

1 The collective wouldn't have been formed if it hadn't been for the terror. In fact given the choice, I wouldn't have joined myself ... But I realised there was a war on and everyone had to make sacrifices ... Once the work groups were established on a friendly basis and worked
5 their own lands, everyone got on well enough together. ... To work in common is by no means stupid. It meant large concentrations of land instead of small, scattered, plots, which saved time and effort. We didn't live worse under collectivisation than before - or only to the extent made inevitable by the war. Those who had had less ... now ate more
10 and better. But no-one went short.

[The speaker] shared, however, the generalised dislike of having to hand over all the produce to the 'pile' and to get nothing but rations in return. Another bad thing was the way the militia columns requisitioned livestock from the collective, issuing vouchers in return ...
15 As elsewhere, the abolition of money soon led to the coining of local money, a task the blacksmith carried out by punching holes in tin disks ... The money was ... distributed ... to collectivists to spend on their 'vices' ... With the money he could go to the café - there were only two left open: one for the collectivists and one for the 'individualists' - and
20 have a cup of coffee - no spirits were served, the bottles had been taken away... [5]

Note the puritanical attitudes, particularly to alcohol, and the separate cafes for collectivised and individual peasants, indicative of the tension between the two groups.

Like the industrial collectives, the agrarian ones were unable to supply the needs of the war economy. Operating as independent self-supporting communities, they were prepared to distribute free food to their favourite militia company, but not to regularly supply the army or the civilians in the towns. In addition, the abolition of money and resort to barter caused real difficulties in relations with the government. Roughly the same quantity of food seems to have been produced as before, so that the main problems lay in supply and transport. Since the Nationalists already controlled most of the grain growing areas at the start of the war and the Republic's food producing area shrank as it lost more territory, the inadequacies of the agrarian collectives were a serious problem. Within a few months the Republic was experiencing severe food shortages and it was hardly surprising that there was soon pressure, as in the case of the industrial collectives, to restore private ownership or introduce state control.

c) An assessment of the collectives

Historians sympathetic to the collectives have argued that they operated for too short a time for definite conclusions to be drawn about their viability and also that their problems cannot be disentangled from the general economic difficulties caused by the war. Collectives functioned in a difficult and often hostile environment where the moderate political parties opposed them and did their best to undermine them, so that the scales were weighted against them. For example, the Communist Minister of Agriculture, Uribe, set up small business and peasant federations specifically to combat collectives.

However, after making all allowances, the general consensus is that, while collectives may have satisfied the aspirations of many of their members, they were not an economic success, and hindered rather than helped the war effort. It was clearly not practical to base an economy, especially in war-time, on a series of self-governing, autonomous communities. Paul Preston concludes that 'war was hardly the best context for massive economic experiments. Collectivisation tended to disrupt both the continuity of production and market mechanisms at precisely the time when planning and co-ordination were most urgently needed'.[6]

3 The Growth of Communist Influence in the Republic and the Debate over Revolution versus the War

a) The rise of the Communists

In July 1936 the Spanish Communist Party (PCE) had only about 40,000 members. A year later it was the main political force in the Republic. By December 1936 its membership was an estimated

250,000, compared with about 160,000 Socialists, 154,000 FAI (Anarchists) and 60,000 POUM members. By October 1937 it had an estimated 400,000 members.

How did the Communists achieve this rapid rise to prominence? Firstly they were bound to benefit from the fact that the USSR was the only foreign power of any note to assist the Republic. Arms and supplies were channelled through the Communist Party, and the International Brigades were also Communist organised and controlled. Aid brought with it an influx of Soviet agents and military advisers, including Koltzov, ostensibly a journalist on *Pravda* (the official Soviet newspaper) but in fact an emissary of Stalin, and Orlov, a leading member of the Soviet secret police. Working behind the scenes, these advisers acquired increasing influence.

Secondly, the Communists took the lead in military re-organisation and in the creation of a Popular Army (see Chapter 6). They gained many members and supporters in the armed forces, including the commanders Lister and Modesto, and General Miaja. Their role in the successful defence of Madrid made them even more prominent. One of their best known members was the great orator Dolores Ibárruri, termed 'La Pasionaria' on account of her stirring speeches.

A third important reason for their growth was their ability to exploit the weaknesses and divisions of the other political parties. They were helped by the fact that the Socialists, anarchists and the POUM all conflicted with one another, and that the Socialists were also split between the followers of Largo Caballero and those of Prieto. The Communists, on the other hand, were a tightly knit and well-disciplined group. Though they were careful not to appear too important and were in the minority in the government, other ministers, such as the Foreign Secretary, Alvarez del Vayo, followed their line or collaborated with them.

Membership of the party was also boosted in 1936 and 1937 by peasants and small businessmen, who saw the Communists as defenders of property rights against the anarchists and POUM. They were also strengthened by the merger, in 1936, of the Communist and Socialist youth movements and of the Catalan Communist and Socialist parties.

b) The ideological debate

From the start the Communists set out to limit the revolution and abolish the collectives. This led them into direct conflict with the anarchists and the POUM, a confrontation which dominated Republican politics from Autumn 1936 to Spring 1937 and was accompanied by an intense and impassioned debate about the relationship between the revolution and the war.

The Communists' case was that any revolution must be postponed until the war had been won. Revolution was seen as a distraction from the main business of winning the war. It also threatened to alienate the middle class and peasants. Given the performance of the collectives, the Communists and their supporters had a number of points on their side. But the major reason why they took an anti-revolutionary line was to follow Soviet foreign policy strategy. The USSR wished to forge an alliance with Britain and France in a front against fascism, but this aim would be thwarted by a revolutionary Spain which would alarm and antagonise the western democracies and increase their hostility to the Soviet Union as well as setting them irrevocably against the Republic. The Communists therefore wanted to present the Republic as a law-abiding democratic regime which deserved the approval of the western powers. They had a further incentive to take a moderate stand since, as a late arrival on the political scene, they had only a limited amount of working-class support compared with the Socialists and anarchists, and so were obliged to look to the middle class and peasants to augment their membership.

While the Communists argued that a revolutionary Republic could not defeat Franco, the anarchists and POUM claimed just the opposite - that revolution was an essential prerequisite of Republican victory. They took the view that revolution would mobilise and enthuse the whole population against the Nationalists, and that a revolutionary war was the best, and indeed the only, means of defeating Franco's superior conventional forces. They argued that the Republic had little to lose by revolution since Britain and France had no intention of assisting it, whatever its political complexion. They attacked the Communists for putting the interests of the USSR before those of Spain.

Where does the balance of this argument lie? Most historians consider that the Communists' economic and military strategy was superior to that of their rivals and though, in the end, this strategy did not win the war, it is difficult to envisage a revolutionary war as being more successful. Such a war, with militia and guerrilla activity, would have been different from the one fought, but would have been unlikely to have ultimately defeated the Nationalists (the military campaigns are covered in Chapter 6). It is, in any event, doubtful if the left-wing groups - anarchists, POUM and left Socialists - could ever have reconciled their differences sufficiently to work together in government. The anarchists, in any case, had always been against state authority and were unprepared for the complexities of the situation into which they were plunged in July 1936.

c) Communist influence in Largo Caballero's Government

Along with Communist influence went greater Soviet intervention, and this began to be increasingly resented by Largo Caballero. Largo initially needed the Communists in order to counter the anti-fascist committees and collectives, but he disliked being given unsolicited advice by Stalin, opposed the proposed merger of the Communist and Socialists Parties which threatened to submerge the latter, and resisted attempts by the Communists to acquire greater control over the army. The extent to which he was fighting an uphill battle against Soviet interference is evident from this altercation with Rosenberg, the Soviet Ambassador, in January 1937:

1 Out you go, out! You must learn, Señor Ambassador, that the Spaniards may be poor and need aid from abroad, but we are sufficiently proud not to accept that a foreign ambassador should try and impose his will on the head of the Spanish government. And as for you, Vayo, you ought
5 to remember that you are a Spaniard and minister of foreign affairs of the republic, instead of arranging to agree with a foreign diplomat to exert pressure on your own Prime Minister.[7]

Early in 1937 he clashed with the Communists when they demanded the removal of General Asensio, the Under Secretary for War. Asensio was blamed for the fall of Málaga in February 1937 and Largo was eventually forced to dismiss him. But this did not save the Prime Minister. By May 1937 prominent members of the government including Azaña the President, Prieto and Negrín, were plotting with the Communists to remove him from office.

4 The Civil War within the Civil War: Fighting between the Political Groups in Barcelona in May 1937

All these tensions came to a head in four days of street fighting in Barcelona in May 1937 which marked a major crisis and turning point in the Republic. The May Days spelt the end of revolution and the establishment of Communist hegemony. In the early months of 1937 Communist attacks on the anarchist CNT and the POUM had increased. The anarchist representatives resigned from the Generalitat in protest against a decree that political parties give up their arms. In April there were clashes on the French frontier between anarchist militias and the government troops sent to take over from them. At the end of April leading UGT and CNT members were assassinated in tit-for-tat killings. The atmosphere in Barcelona was very different from the heady days of the summer revolution.

On 3 May an internal civil war erupted. The catalyst was an attempt by Assault Guards, commanded by the PSUC Police Commissioner, to take over the Barcelona telephone exchange from the CNT. The exchange was an important centre of communications and the anarchist eavesdropping and censoring of phone calls had been a long-standing irritant. The CNT resisted, and fighting broke out between the anarchists and the POUM on the one side and the Catalan Communist/Socialist Party on the other. Barricades were thrown up, the opposing Republican groups fired on one another from their respective headquarters in the centre of the city and a general strike was called.

However, the CNT and POUM were at a disadvantage, since, due to ideological differences, they could not agree on concerted action. Also the anarchist leaders in the Madrid Government were urging the Barcelona CNT to back down. Owing to these divisions the fighting soon petered out as additional government troops from Valencia arrived to restore order. In all, between 200 and 500 people were killed.

The May Days resulted in a decisive shift in the balance of power in favour of the Communists and their allies. The main political casualty was Largo Caballero, who by this time was being described by the Communists as 'a burnt-out trades union boss.'[8] In April a Communist Party executive meeting, attended by Soviet representatives, had already decided to replace him with the Finance Minister, Juan Negrín. When Largo resisted pressure to suppress the POUM his fate was sealed. Azaña and Prieto turned against him and he had no alternative but to resign.

Negrín, the Communists' choice as the new Prime Minister, was a former professor of physiology, not previously very prominent, though he had been an efficient finance minister in Largo's government. He was chosen mainly for his anti-revolutionary and pro-Communist views. Unlike the austere Largo he was an expansive and pleasure-loving individual. His Cabinet was based on middle of the road Republicans and right-wing Socialists, and excluded the anarchists. Though still in a minority in the Cabinet, the Communists now wielded increased political and military power.

5 Negrín's Government, May 1937 to March 1939

Historians have taken widely differing views of Negrín, seeing him either as a pawn of the Communists or alternatively as an astute statesman, trying to perform 'a delicate and dangerous balancing act'[9] between Soviet and Spanish interests, while at the same time doing his best to mobilise the population behind the war. The Nationalist cartoon on page 55 caricatures Negrín's subservience to Stalin, who is depicted riding on Negrín's back, driving and manipulating him. What is certain is that Negrín felt he had little option but to acquiesce in a large degree of Communist control if Spain was to continue to receive the Soviet military aid necessary to enable the Republic to continue the war.

Under Negrín the Republic was more united than under Largo Caballero, but it was also more dictatorial. Dissent was not tolerated and press censorship increased. The Cortes met less and less frequently, becoming a rubber stamp. In October 1937 Largo was removed from the executive committee of the UGT and forbidden to speak at public meetings. Catalan autonomy was greatly reduced, the Generalitat ignored and Companys sidelined. The last vestiges of revolution disappeared as the collectives were dismantled. In August 1937, the Council of Aragon, the last bastion of the anarchists, was dissolved and Ascaso and other leaders arrested. The CNT, preoccupied with internal disputes, declined.

The POUM was the Communists' main victim. Its publications were banned and its leader, Nin, was kidnapped and, as was later discovered, tortured and killed. Forged documents were produced, claiming to show that POUM members were agents of Franco. By 1938, there were 3,000 political prisoners in Republican Spain, and

'Resist! Resist! Stalin's watchword to Negrín.'
Negrín's dependence on the Soviet government is satirised in this cartoon

foreigners like Orwell, who were sympathetic to the POUM, only escaped from the country with difficulty. Negrín acquiesced in this suppression which was carried out by the SIM (from its initials), a Soviet dominated secret police force with its own prisons and camps. The SIM set up special tribunals to try political offences at show trials, where opponents were accused of being fascist spies. It inaugurated a mini reign of terror, a Spanish version of the purges which were occurring in this period in the USSR. Ironically most of the Russians in Spain were themselves to be purged on their return to the Soviet Union.

Prieto, the Defence Minister, who had intrigued with the Communists to oust Largo Caballero, soon fell foul of them in turn. Like Largo, he tried to reduce Communist influence in the army and was disillusioned by their persecution of the POUM. As a result he was blamed for the defeat at Teruel (see pages 88-9), accused of defeatism about the outcome of the war and removed from the Cabinet in April 1938.

Negrín's slogan was 'to resist is to win', his aim being to prolong the war as long as possible hoping for the outbreak of general European conflict which might bring in Britain and France on his side. In May 1938 when the position of the Republic seemed hopeless, he set out his pre-conditions for a compromise peace in a moderate 13 point programme designed to appeal to the western democracies: he promised the withdrawal of foreign troops and respect for property rights and religious freedom. But it fell on deaf ears in the west and even more so in Nationalist Spain, where Franco would consider nothing but unconditional surrender.

With the fall of Catalonia in January 1939 the Republic held only the territory between Valencia and Madrid, and Negrín's policy of continuing to fight on against the odds lost the support of all the political groups except the Communists. He became increasingly isolated and in March 1939 Colonel Casado led a military coup against him in Madrid (see page 91). This second civil war within the Civil War re-played all the political conflicts which had plagued the Republic in the previous three years. It did not, however, prevent the inevitable Nationalist victory. By the end of March 1939 the war was over and the remaining Republican politicians fled into exile, there to blame one another for their defeat.

6 Daily life in Republican Spain

a) Economic and social conditions

As the war went on, life in the Republic was increasingly characterised by economic hardship. There were shortages of food and of almost all consumer goods. Food prices in Barcelona more than trebled in the course of the war, while wages rose by only 15 per cent. The following table of Catalan economic statistics[10] illustrates the rise in prices and unemployment and the fall in production in the first year of the war:

Prices and Unemployment in Catalonia			
Date	Industrial production	Unemployment	Prices
Jan. 1936	100	55,288	169
June 1936	98	72,782	172
Jan. 1937	70	91,416	224
June 1937	68	79,404	304

Rationing was introduced and there were long queues in the shops and a thriving black market. Meat and eggs disappeared, and vegetables such as lentils, 'Dr.Negrín's resistance pills', became a prominent feature of the daily diet. The Republic was being slowly starved. Overcrowding in the cities was exacerbated by the numbers of refugees fleeing from the advancing Nationalists. Also, in the cities, there was the ever present threat of air raids.

Within these constraints, the Republic did try to introduce some social reforms. Priority was given to education, with 1,000 new secular schools being opened in 1937 and military schools established to teach recruits how to read and write. Family allowances, accident and illness insurance were also introduced along with a free health service and child-welfare clinics. Most of these reforms, however, could never be properly implemented due to the problems of the war.

b) The position of women

One of the most significant changes brought about by the revolution of 1936 was in the status of women. Even under the Second Republic, long-standing patriarchal attitudes, reinforced by religion, had ensured that women occupied an inferior position whether in the family or at work. Now, equal legal status, civil marriage, divorce and abortion were introduced. Some militiamen and women even got married in specially designed 'revolutionary' secular ceremonies. There was greater social freedom, for example unmarried girls going around unchaperoned. More women worked, some in jobs in industry and transport vacated by the men conscripted into the army. A few women rose to political prominence, notably Dolores Ibárruri, the Communist leader, and Federica Montseny, the anarchist who became the first woman Cabinet member. Political parties set up women's organisations which engaged in debate and propaganda. Some women even joined the militias, though few were involved in action at the front, and they were restricted to ancillary roles from 1937.

However, as well as being of short duration, most of these changes did not impact very greatly on the daily lives of most women. For example, women continued to be paid less than men, even in collectives. In this extract a female CNT member observes that male attitudes had not fundamentally changed:

1   It was marvellous ... to live in a collective, a free society where one could say what one thought, where if the village committee seemed unsatisfactory one could say so. The committee took no big decisions without calling the whole village together in a general assembly. All this
5   was wonderful. But the role of women - that hadn't changed. There was much talk but little action.
    The men were sincerely dedicated to furthering the revolution, but they didn't understand that the revolution had to be made in depth, at all levels. The revolution has to begin at home. In truth, the question of
10 women's liberation wasn't posed as part of the revolutionary process, at least not in my experience. Perhaps things were different in Catalonia, but in Aragon the woman's place was in the kitchen or working the land. [11]

Inevitably, the political move to the right from 1937 and the preoccupation with winning the war, meant that the position of women became a lower priority.

c) Terror and repression

As in most civil wars, terror directed against opponents was an integral feature of life in both the Republican and Nationalist zones. But unlike Nationalist Spain, where terror was official policy from the start, in the Republic it was initially the result of spontaneous action by left-wing groups and militias who took the law into their own hands. Immediately following the defeat of the rising in July 1936 unofficial revolutionary courts were set up which summarily tried and condemned to death anyone who could be shown to have anti-Republican or right-wing views. Membership or support of the Falange or CEDA invariably guaranteed a death sentence, but victims were often arbitrarily denounced and many personal as well as political scores were settled. Those condemned would be literally 'taken for a ride', the *paseo* as it was termed, involved being transported by car or truck outside the town, shot and left by the roadside. Sometimes trials were dispensed with altogether and the car would arrive with no warning at the victim's home late at night to carry him off. This eyewitness account by an American journalist describes the *paseos* in Madrid in Summer 1936:

1   Many mornings after breakfast ... I used to make the rounds of the outskirts of Madrid to check up on the *paseo* victims of the night before.
    Singly and in clusters they lay alongside the roadway, riddled with bullets ... Some of the victims were lined up against a wall in firing-squad

5 style. Others were told to run and were shot down like rabbits as they
zigzagged away ... During the first weeks the death-carts did not come
around to collect these bodies until nearly noon. Later, they started at
dawn and had them all removed by 8 o'clock in the morning ... As the
death-carts lumbered towards the morgue, the feet of the stacked dead
10 sticking out the rear ... men and women would fall in line behind them
and follow them to the death house to see if a friend or relative were
among the victims ... I went once with another newspaperman. I shall
not forget the scrawny old morgue-keeper and her toothless grin as she
cackled: 'business is poor, boys, only eighty today.'[12]

These killings were not officially condoned and by September 1936
Largo Caballero's government had succeeded in replacing the unofficial courts with 'Peoples' Tribunals'. From December 1936 no death
sentence could be carried out until confirmed by four judges and by
the Cabinet. This, however, did not prevent the executions from
continuing and there were further waves of repression, for example
the killing of hundreds of prisoners in Madrid in November 1936,
when it was expected that the capital would fall to the Nationalists and
that a 'fifth column' (a term coined by Mola) of Francoists in the city
would rise up and help deliver it to the besieging army. In all, it is estimated that upwards of 55,000 opponents were killed in the
Republican zone during the war and many pro-Nationalists who
found themselves there were obliged to spend the war in hiding, some
taking refuge in foreign embassies.

From 1937 the terror against the right subsided, but was replaced
by a Communist terror against their political opponents on the left
(as described on pages 55-6).

7 How Did the Political Problems of the Republic Contribute to its Defeat in the War?

There has been much debate among historians about the impact of
the internal politics of the Republic on the outcome of the war. One
issue is whether Communist ascendancy benefited the Republic or
not. Most historians take the view that the Communists, despite their
repressive methods, were better at fighting the war than their more
left-wing opponents. Centralising policies and autocratic measures
certainly antagonised and demoralised large sections of the population and some members of the International Brigades went home
disillusioned with their experiences. But as Paul Preston points out,
'The Republic lost far more territory in the first ten months of the war
before the Communists had finally established their hegemony than it
did in the subsequent twenty-three months during which they dominated the war effort.'[13]

There is a more general sense, however, in which the Communists may be said to have acted against the interests of the Republic. This was because of their willingness to follow the lead of the USSR and its agents in Spain, who came to play a major role in decision making. The exact degree of Soviet influence in Spanish affairs is difficult to assess, but it was certainly substantial and contrasts with the much smaller amount exerted by Germany and Italy in the Nationalist zone. The Communists, in following the Soviet line, were subordinating the interests of the Republic to those of the Soviet Union. These interests were by no means the same - Stalin was helping the Republic as a means to achieve his own foreign policy objectives and he reduced aid in the last year of the war when involvement in Spain no longer served his purpose.

Quite apart from the merits or demerits of Communist influence, a major political failing of the Republic was the inability of the diverse political groups within it to sink their differences in order to form a common front against the enemy, a willingness which was much more apparent in the Nationalist zone. Republicans were sharply divided over what they were fighting for, whether for the political institutions of the Second Republic or for a revolution. The first year of the war was dominated by internal conflict and even when the moderate elements gained the upper hand after the May Days, the defeated groups were never reconciled.

Success in war requires strong leadership, and this was perhaps the respect in which the Republic contrasts most unfavourably with Nationalist Spain. Neither Largo Caballero nor Negrín was able to impose his authority or establish effective control over both military and civil matters in the manner of Franco. It can, of course, be argued that the political problems of the Republic were aggravated by military failure, just as those in Nationalist Spain were mitigated by success.

The internal problems of the Republic were not the only reasons for its defeat, but they must be regarded as a significant component of it. As Paul Heywood points out, 'Division on the Republican side, exacerbated by the role of the Soviet Union, was a crucial factor in the ultimate defeat of the Republic' [14]

References

1   Quoted in Raymond Carr, *The Spanish Tragedy* (Weidenfeld & Nicolson, 1977), p.91.
2   George Orwell, *Homage to Catalonia* (Martin, Secker & Warburg, 1970), pp.16-17.
3   Ronald Fraser, *Blood of Spain* (Penguin, 1981), pp.214-15.
4   J.M. Blazquez, *I helped build an army* (Secker & Warburg, 1939), pp.167-70.
5   Fraser, *Blood of Spain*, pp.360-61.
6   Paul Preston, *A concise history of the Spanish Civil War* (Fontana Press, 1996), p.177.

7   Quoted in Hugh Thomas, *The Spanish Civil War* (Penguin, 1990), pp.533-34.
8   Raymond Carr, *The Spanish Tragedy*, p.114.
9   Ibid, p.198
10   Stanley Payne, *The Spanish Revolution* (Weidenfeld & Nicolson, 1970), p.257.
11   Fraser, *Blood of Spain*, p.288.
12   Quoted in Harry Browne, *Spain's Civil War* (Longman, 1996), pp.115-16.
13   Paul Preston, *Concise history of the Spanish Civil War*, p.171.
14   Paul Heywood, 'Why the Republic lost' in *History Today*, March 1989, p.27.

Summary Diagram
Republican Spain from July 1936 to March 1939

Republican governments and main political events from July 1936 to March 1939

<u>Prime Ministers</u>

July to September 1936	Casares Quiroga Martiñez Barrio Giral	Summer 1936 Revolution Militias formed Collectives set up
September 1936 to May 1937	Largo Caballero	Communist influence increased Conflict between Communists/Socialists and anarchists/POUM over revolution versus the War Collectives discouraged Fighting in Barcelona in May 1937
May 1937 to March 1939	Negrín	Communist and Soviet domination POUM and anarchists suppressed Collectives dismantled March 1939, Casado coup in Madrid

The problems of the Republic

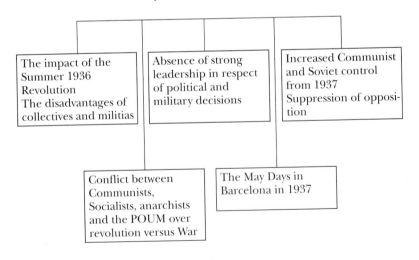

The impact of the Summer 1936 Revolution
The disadvantages of collectives and militias

Absence of strong leadership in respect of political and military decisions

Increased Communist and Soviet control from 1937
Suppression of opposition

Conflict between Communists, Socialists, anarchists and the POUM over revolution versus War

The May Days in Barcelona in 1937

5 Foreign Powers and the War

1 Introduction: the European powers in 1936

The Civil War was largely fought by Spaniards, but it was foreign assistance to both sides which sustained it over a three year period. Spanish industry simply did not have the capacity to produce the required amounts of aircraft, tanks, or even armaments and munitions, most of which had to be supplied from abroad. Even with foreign help, the war has been described as 'a pauper's war', fought with limited and often outdated and inefficient weapons.

As a dramatic example of the ideological conflicts of the 1930s, the war was bound to generate considerable interest outside Spain. The main European powers responded to it partly in ideological terms, but primarily in relation to their wider diplomatic aims. All the powers involved were mainly concerned as to how they could turn events in Spain to their own advantage.

In the Summer of 1936, the German and Italian dictatorships were in the ascendancy in Europe. Mussolini had just completed the successful, though expensive, conquest of Abyssinia, in his endeavour to make Italy great, feared and respected. The League of Nations had imposed economic sanctions against Italy but these had proved ineffective and, combined with the League's unwillingness to condemn Japan in the 1931 Manchurian crisis, had finally discredited it as a peace keeping agency. In defiance of the Versailles Treaty, Hitler had introduced German re-armament in 1935. Taking advantage of the preoccupation of Britain and France with Abyssinia, he proceeded in March 1936 to remilitarise the Rhineland, a move which brought increased prestige and an improved strategic position in relation to France.

The extent of Hitler's expansionist ambitions to acquire living space in eastern Europe was not appreciated by Britain and France in 1936: they tended to take at face value his public protestations that he was merely seeking to revise the Versailles Settlement. But in any case, the two western European democracies were on the defensive. In Britain, the predominantly Conservative National Government was eager above all to avoid another European conflict. Britain could not afford another major war, given the economic problems resulting from the 1929-33 Depression and her world-wide imperial defence commitments. The political and military consensus was that Britain must at all costs avoid simultaneous conflict with her three potential enemies, Germany, Italy, and Japan in the Far East. The National Government had therefore already embarked on a policy of conciliation or appeasement, especially directed towards Italy in an attempt to detach her from a possible German alliance. But by 1936 this policy had not succeeded. In the Abyssinian crisis of 1935-6 Britain's contradictory strategies, of upholding the authority of the League while at the same time making concessions to the Italians, had both failed. The only effects had been to irretrievably weaken the League while at the same time antagonising Mussolini, with the result that the April 1935 Stresa Front, formed by Britain, France and Italy to counter the German threat, had collapsed, and Mussolini had begun to move closer to Hitler.

France had more to fear than Britain from the growth of German power in Europe. But, since the end of the First World War, French influence had declined. French governments were generally weak, short-lived coalitions, and France was plagued with political divisions and economic and social problems. Her military strategy was based on defence rather than attack, as exemplified by the Maginot fortification line along the German frontier. Because of these weaknesses, France tended to follow the British lead in foreign policy, rather than pursue an independent course. This was partly why she had taken no action over the German re-occupation of the Rhineland.

Since the coming to power of Hitler in 1933, Soviet foreign policy had been largely devoted to a search for security against the threat of German eastwards expansion at the expense of Slavs and other so-called 'inferior' races. This security was best achieved by an alliance with Britain and France which would encircle Germany. Therefore, the traditional Soviet support for world revolution was being played down in 1936 in favour of Popular Front alliances between Communists and other anti-fascist parties. But Stalin found this policy difficult to pursue - British governments remained hostile to communism, and the 1935 alliance with France was filled with loopholes. Stalin obviously wished the Spanish Republican government to remain in power, thereby adding to the strength of the anti-German bloc, but his first concern in 1936 was to improve relations with the Western democracies, lest he should be left to face Germany alone.

It was in this context that the five main European powers decided their attitude to the conflict in Spain.

2 German Aid to the Nationalists

On his arrival in Morocco, Franco's most pressing problem, given the presence in the Mediterranean of the pro-Republican Spanish navy, was how to transport the army of Africa to mainland Spain. Germany and Italy were the most likely sources of aid. Both Franco and Mola petitioned the German Foreign Office but the Foreign Minister, Neurath, was disinclined to help, favouring a cautious approach. The Foreign Office took the view that the Nationalists were unlikely to win. But Franco meantime had decided to bypass the official channels in favour of a direct approach to Hitler. On 23 July 1936 he sent Bernhardt and Langenheim, two German businessmen based in Morocco, to Germany. From Berlin, Hess, the Deputy Führer, directed them to Bayreuth, where Hitler was attending a Wagner festival. When they met Hitler on the evening of 25 July he was in a euphoric mood, having just enjoyed a performance of 'Siegfried'. Disregarding the views of the Foreign Office, he immediately made a decision to aid the Nationalists, sending twenty transport planes, which, arriving on 29 July, were to be the first instalment of substantial aid.

Various reasons have been put forward to explain Hitler's decision to assist the Nationalists. At the Nuremberg trials in 1945, Goering claimed that the chief motive was to use Spain as a testing ground for the German air force, but this seems to have been a very minor reason. Hitler's thinking, it is now believed, had much more to do with promoting a favourable balance of power in western Europe and using a Nationalist-run Spain to weaken France, thus facilitating German expansionist moves in Eastern Europe. His main aim was to prevent the emergence of a French-Spanish bloc which might be directed against Germany.

By co-operating with Italy in aiding the Nationalists, Hitler also intended to improve relations with Mussolini and finally detach him from Britain and France. This aspect of his policy is explained in the following report from the German Ambassador in Rome in December 1936:

1 Germany has in my opinion every reason for being gratified if Italy continues to interest herself deeply in the Spanish affair ... The struggle for dominant political influence in Spain lays bare the natural opposition between Italy and France; at the same time the position of Italy as
5 a power in the western Mediterranean comes into competition with that of Britain. All the more clearly will Italy recognise the advisability of confronting the Western powers shoulder to shoulder with Germany... 1

A secondary motive for German intervention was economic, to acquire from Spain the raw materials which were essential for German re-armament.

German help to Franco comprised planes, tanks and munitions, rather than troops. The chief German contribution, after the airlift, was the Condor Legion, which arrived in Spain in November 1936 in time to take part in the battles around Madrid. This was a combined air, tank and artillery unit, with between 100 and 600 aircraft, fighters and bombers and 10,000 men, which was kept up to strength for the duration of the war and played an important role in the campaigns of 1937 and 1938.

3 Italian Aid to the Nationalists

Franco also sought help from Mussolini, sending Luis Bolín, who had made the arrangements for his Canaries-Morocco flight, to Rome for this purpose. On 22 July 1936 Bolín gained an audience with Ciano, the Italian Foreign Minister. Ciano was enthusiastic, but Mussolini was at first inclined to refuse. He only changed his mind a few days later, after further representations from General Mola and the Spanish monarchists, who had had some previous contacts with the Italian government. Mussolini was also influenced by news of French aid to the Republic which he wished to counter, and at the end of July he sent 12 Savoia bombers to Morocco.

In spite of his initial ambivalence, Mussolini quickly became extremely enthusiastic about helping the Nationalists and committed considerably more military resources, in financial terms, than Germany. From the end of 1936, there were about 45,000 Italian troops (theoretically volunteers) in Spain at any one time, amounting to 60,000 in all, in addition to planes, tanks and munitions.

Mussolini was looking for new military success following his Abyssinian adventure and his aims were more grandiose than those of Hitler. In addition to reducing French power, he dreamt of re-establishing a Mediterranean Roman Empire and of reducing Spain to a satellite fascist state which would be dependent on Italy. As a reward for his efforts he hoped to acquire the Balearic Islands as a permanent naval base. Mussolini explained his objectives in a conversation with Ciano in November 1937:

> 1   First of all we have spent about four and a half milliards [thousand million] in Spain ... German expenditure according to what Goering said is in the region of three and a half milliards. We wish to be paid and must be paid. But there is also, over and above that, a political aspect.
> 5   We want Nationalist Spain which has been saved by virtue of all manner of Italian and German aid to remain closely associated with our manoeuvres ... Rome and Berlin must therefore keep in close contact so as to act in such a way that Franco will always follow our policy ... We have established at Palma a naval and air base; we keep ships perma-
> 10 nently stationed there and have three airfields. We intend to remain in that situation as long as possible. In any case, Franco must come to understand that, even after our eventual evacuation, Majorca must remain an Italian base in the event of a war with France.[2]

None of this came to pass. Not only was the performance of the Italian troops disappointing, but Franco was adept at avoiding repaying his obligations to his allies.

In November 1936 Germany and Italy both recognised Franco's regime in anticipation of an early capture of Madrid by the Nationalists, and continued to support him for the remainder of the war.

4 The French and British Response to the War

Just as the two fascist dictatorships were natural allies of Franco, so France was the state most likely to aid the Republic. A Franco alliance with Germany and Italy would surround France with enemies and a

Nationalist Spain could disrupt communications with the French colonies in North Africa. In July 1936 France, like Spain, had a Popular Front government and the French Prime Minister, León Blum was a Socialist.

On 19 July Spain's Prime Minister Giral sent a request to France for aircraft and armaments. On 20 July the French Government decided to help and on 22 July agreed to send 20 bombers and other arms. The next day Blum and the Foreign Minister, Delbos, set off for London for a pre-arranged conference with the British government. When they returned to Paris on 24 July they were greeted with the news that aid to the Republic was about to be publicised and attacked in the right-wing press. Divisions now appeared in the Cabinet with the Radical members beginning to argue against aid. It was this, combined with absence of support from Britain, which led the French government on 25 July to reverse its decision, though private sales of arms could still be made. Some arms and aircraft did slip through, amounting to about 70 planes by 7 August, but meantime the French government began working on a non-intervention scheme. On 7 August Blum definitely opted for non-intervention.

Denial of French aid was a great blow to the Republic, obliging it to rely on the Soviet Union as its sole means of support, and historians have debated the reasons for Blum's change of policy. It used to be generally believed that the French government's decision was largely due to British pressure being brought to bear during his visit to London on 23-24 July and during Admiral Darlan's visit on 3 August. Hugh Thomas, for example, considers that:

1   fear of offending England was the main reason why the French Cabinet was thus brought on the 8 August to reverse its decision. [Darlan had been told on 3 August by his British counterpart, that] '... there was no point in making any approach to Britain about Spain, and, further that
5   Franco was a "good Spanish patriot" ... Nothing should be done which allowed the spread of communism to Spain or, even worse, to Portugal.'[3]

The argument that the French were influenced by Britain is supported by the fact that throughout the inter-war period French foreign policy generally followed Britain's lead rather than the reverse. However, there are also arguments to show that Blum's decision might have been as much, or even more, due to French internal problems. The extremes of public opinion on the right and left led to fears that aid to the Republic would precipitate unrest and even civil war in France. French Catholics were also opposed to helping the anti-religious Republicans. All this made the Radicals in the Cabinet unwilling to agree to aid.

The following sources provide different interpretations of French policy and of the attitude of the British government. In this extract the Spanish envoy in Paris attributes Blum's change of mind on 25 July 1936 to domestic concerns:

1 Last night [24 July] I was urgently summoned by the Leader of the
Government to his house, where I found four Ministers ... At their
request I made a few considerations upon the character of the Spanish
struggle, which cannot be looked upon as being strictly national owing
5 to a series of reasons which we analysed; military frontier in the
Pyrenees, Balearic Isles, Straits of Gibraltar, Canaries and breakage of the
political unity of Western Europe. Duty therefore and direct interest on
the part of France to help us. How? We examined our demands and,
from the attitude of the Ministers, I gathered that there existed a diver-
10 gence of opinion...
   When I went this morning [25 July] to the Air Ministry everything
was going well; when I arrived at the Potez [aircraft] firm the difficulties
seemed insurmountable ... When Blum went this morning to see the
President of the Republic, he found him perturbed and in such a state
15 of mind that he said, 'what is being planned, this delivery of armaments
to Spain, may mean war or revolution in France.'
   The position of the President of the Republic is shared by several
Ministers: the Cabinet was divided in its views and the President of the
Chamber, Herriot, has seen Blum and begged him to reflect, for he
20 considered that this has never been done before, and that it may justify
a *de facto* [deriving from the actual situation as opposed to theoretical
rights] recognition by Germany and Italy of any semblance of government set up in a Spanish city and provide it with arms and ammunition
in greater quantities than those France can supply. From half-past two
25 till a quarter-to four I have been with the Prime Minister ... 'My soul is
torn,' said Blum, 'I shall maintain my position at all costs and in spite of
all risks,' he said. 'We must help Spain that is friendly to us. How? We
shall see.'
   At 3.30 I again met some of them: the fight had been stern. ... The
30 resolution of the Cabinet has been to avoid delivery from Government
to Government, but to grant us the necessary permits so that private
industry may deliver to us ...[4]

On the other hand the American Ambassador in Paris subscribed to
the view that British pressure was responsible for the French decision:

1 The reasons which led to the decision were communicated to the
Embassy by a reliable press contact who obtained his information from
a member of the French Supreme War Council. According to this infor-
mant certain members of the Blum Cabinet particularly Cot, Air
5 Minister, decided on 21 July to accede to a request from Spain to send
arms and ammunition urgently required by the Madrid Government ...
On 22 July Corbin, French Ambassador in London, telephoned Blum
personally and called to his attention that the British Government was
extremely worried about this contingency. Corbin urged Blum to come
10 over and discuss the situation with Baldwin and Eden as soon as
possible ... In London Eden drew Blum's attention to the grave inter-

national consequences which might result from French active support of
the Madrid Government. The fears of the British Government were
strengthened by a report from the French military Intelligence which
15 indicated a certain movement of German troops on the French eastern
border ... Blum returned to Paris on the 25th and immediately called
the Cabinet Council meeting mentioned above, in the course of which
the British point of view was brought forcibly to the attention of his
extremist colleagues, particularly Cot. After a lengthy debate the more
20 moderate elements, Blum, Daladier and Delbos, who advocated a policy
of strict neutrality, won out.[5]

After the War Blum recalled a conversation with Eden in London on
23 July :

In the hall of Claridge's Hotel, Eden asked 'Are you going to send arms
to the Spanish Republic?' 'Yes' said Blum. 'It is your affair,' Eden replied,
'but I ask you one thing. Be prudent.'[6]

In his memoirs, however, Eden denied influencing the French
government. In his account of a meeting with Corbin, the French
Ambassador, on 28 August,

1   I [said] I had been much intrigued at the story ... brought back from
Paris that the suggestion of non-intervention was not originally French
but British. I had said that there was of course no truth in this, though
I had always thought M. Blum's initiative a wise one. The Ambassador
5   remarked that, so far as he could recollect, there had been no discussion of the Spanish problem during our three-power meeting. That is
also my own recollection and the evidence of the records in London.[7]

In the event, the French frontier was closed to arms and volunteers
and France opted for non-intervention. The frontier was re-opened
briefly in March 1938 as a result of the Austrian and Czech crises
which threatened European war, but closed again in June 1938 when
the Socialists were ousted from the French Cabinet. The concessions
to Hitler at Munich removed the last prospect of French assistance to
the Republic.

While the French government vacillated, the British government
had determined from the start to avoid involvement in Spain. On 31
July it decided to ban all arms shipments to either side. British
thinking was influenced by several factors. Prime Minister Baldwin's
main concern was to localise the conflict and prevent it spreading and
becoming a general European war. To support the Republic would
offend Italy, with whom Britain was trying to improve relations.
Strategic issues were important, especially the need to preserve
British power in the western Mediterranean and control of Gibraltar.
There were also economic considerations - British investments in
Spain amounted to about £40 million - though these were not the
decisive factor.

Though strategic interests were most important in determining the government's policy, anti-Communism also played a role. Many members of the Government considered that the Republic was too left-wing and too pro-Communist. The general view was that Franco, as a Spanish nationalist, would be a useful bulwark against Communism and might even turn out to be more pro-British than pro-German or pro-Italian. However, in the later stages of the war, the case for supporting the Republic gained some ground since Nationalist success would weaken France, and bolster Germany and Italy, encouraging them in further aggression. On the whole, however, the aim was neutrality with a bias towards the Nationalists.

5 Soviet Aid to the Republic

Stalin too, initially favoured non-intervention. Events in Spain were an inconvenient distraction from domestic problems and diplomatic strategy. But at the end of August 1936, when it became clear that Germany and Italy were supplying the Nationalists, he changed his mind. On 26 August Alexander Orlov, a high-ranking NKVD (secret police) officer, was appointed as the chief Soviet advisor to the Spanish government, and the first Soviet arms arrived in October, in time to play a vital part in the defence of Madrid. By November, there were about 500 Soviet advisors in Spain. Soviet aid was not provided free, and had to be paid for by the transfer to Moscow in October 1936 of the entire Spanish gold reserve. 'They will never see their gold again, just as they do not see their own ears,' Stalin is supposed to have commented, accurately as it turned out.

Stalin's motive was not to promote Communist revolution in Spain, but to prevent any weakening in the position of France, which was an ally of the USSR. His policies were in fact the mirror image of those of Hitler - to help the Republic survive so as to promote a French-Spanish bloc which, linked with Britain, would curtail German expansion. However, the growing Communist influence in Spain was to negate this objective since it antagonised Britain and made a Soviet-British rapprochement less likely.

Soviet aid was at first a considerable asset to the Republic, but from 1938 it was reduced. By this time the Republic was clearly losing the war despite Soviet help. Munich convinced Stalin that he had little to hope for from Britain or France, and he also needed to divert Soviet resources to the Far East in order to counter the Japanese threat.

Apart from Soviet aid, limited French supplies and the International Brigades (described in section 6 below), only Mexico offered (minimal) assistance to the Republic. The Spanish government therefore was at a disadvantage, having to resort to the often overpriced, open market, to purchase many of its armaments.

6 The International Brigades

The idea of an international force of volunteers to fight for the Republic was initiated by Thorez, the French Communist Party secretary, and agreed at a Comintern (the Communist International organisation of world Communist parties) meeting in July, before Stalin had become committed to direct Soviet assistance. The first recruits were foreigners who happened to be in Spain when the rebellion broke out. They were quickly joined by others from a variety of countries. Altogether the brigades totalled about 35,000 men, comprising the following nationalities:

The Composition of the International Brigades	
French	10,000
German/Austrian	5,000
Polish	5,000
Italian	3,350
American	2,800
British	2,000
Canadian	1,000
Yugoslavian	1,500
Hungarian	1,000
Czech	1,500
Scandinavian	1,000

Memoirs written by British members of the brigades often give the impression that most volunteers were upper or middle-class intellectuals. Several such individuals certainly went to Spain, some due to pro-communist sympathies or anti-establishment attitudes, or simply caught up in the excitement of the occasion, as described in this extract:

1   [Giles Romilly] was up at Oxford and hated it ... He telephoned me ... Should we join the International Brigade? All over the country hundreds were being enrolled. I arranged to meet him in Hyde Park the next day ...
    I told him I would go with him as soon as possible ... He had already
5   joined the Communist Party in Oxford; our passports were up to date. He became elated, in full flight ... 'They will take us on. I have been trained in an OTC [officers' training corps], you are an ex-guardsman. Both of us can now fight in a militia. We shall have the right to question any orders with which we don't agree.' He shook his fist at Mayfair
10 where his mother was playing bridge.[8]

However, the upper class were not a majority of the brigades. Most volunteers were industrial workers and the hard core of the brigades were political refugees from Italy, Germany and eastern Europe, who were eager to strike a blow against fascism. Most of the British members were working-class men from the industrial areas which had been badly hit by the depression.

Volunteers came from a variety of left-wing groups, but the Communist Party predominated and the brigades were led by Communists. A system was set up whereby recruits from Britain, posing as tourists, travelled to Paris, where arrangements were made by the Comintern's office to smuggle them across the Pyrenees into Spain. There they received an enthusiastic reception as they proceeded to the training base at Albacete near Valencia. Since they were in Spain unofficially, members of the brigades found it in practice very difficult to leave if they changed their minds or became disillusioned. Most had no prior military training or experience, though a few had fought in the First World War, and the reality of life in the Albacete training camp often proved less romantic than expected. Modern automatic weapons, or guns of any sort, were in short supply. This account by a British volunteer illustrates the flavour of life at the training camp:

1   Morning parade took place on the village square with proper military ceremonial after which the Battalion was stood as ease for the daily pep talk by ... the political commissar. Every day without fail he opened his piece with 'Comrades, the position is as follows ...', continued by a
5   tirade of incredible nonsense, after which we were marched off on the vaguest and most ineffectual field-day manoeuvres ever seen, especially as we had no firearms of any sort. ... But despite the rain and the mud and the general unreality of the whole thing, everybody did their best and remained fairly cheerful.[9]

Notice the reference in the text to political commissars, specially appointed officers whose role was to boost the morale of the troops by emphasising the political goals for which they were fighting.

Eventually five separate International Brigades were formed. Though a small proportion of the total Republican army, they played an important role in most major battles including the defence of Madrid and the Ebro offensive in 1938. It is estimated that approximately 5,000 of these volunteers were killed in the war.

In contrast to the Republicans, there were very few volunteers on the Nationalist side, the exception being a small Irish contingent.

7 The Working of the Non-intervention Committee

This Committee was agreed in August 1936 and it first met in London in early September, chaired by Lord Plymouth, a British diplomat. Twenty-nine countries signed the non-intervention agreement but the Committee almost totally failed in its objectives. It has generally been denigrated as institutionalised hypocrisy or at best described in Eden's words as 'a leaky dam, but better than no dam at all'.[10]

It can be argued that the whole basis of the Committee was flawed since the practical effect of non-intervention was to deny the legitimate government in Spain the right to obtain arms, thereby placing it on the same footing as its opponents who were technically rebels. However, even judged on its own terms, the Committee had little success. It aimed to enforce an embargo on arms to Spain, to ban volunteers and to effect their withdrawal. But although Germany, Italy, the USSR and Portugal - whose assistance as a channel for arms to the Nationalists was considerable - were members, they blatantly contravened the Committee's decisions and undermined it. The USSR also ignored the non-intervention agreement with the justification that Germany and Italy were doing likewise.

The Committee had no real power to prevent intervention in Spain. One reason for this was that it had no legal force or international standing and was dependent on the voluntary compliance of its members. Issues could only be raised by members, and therefore the Republic was unable to bring up any concerns except through intermediaries. Meetings of the Committee were largely taken up with acrimonious accusations and counter-accusations and little progress was made. Various schemes such as posting observers at ports and frontiers were put forward but were mostly ineffectual.

The most successful initiative of the Committee was probably the Nyon Conference agreement in September 1937. In the Summer of 1937 Italian submarines in the Mediterranean began attacking merchant shipping bound for Spain, and the Nyon Conference established naval patrols to prevent this, in which ironically Italy, 'the pirate now turned policeman', as Ciano gleefully put it, was to participate. [11] However, the patrols did limit the submarine attacks.

Non-intervention was also the policy followed by President Roosevelt's government in the United States. This accorded with the American inter-war policy of isolation, embodied in the 1935 Neutrality Act, which forbade the sale of arms by Americans to any state involved in war. Civil wars were not exactly covered by this Act, but in January 1937 a specific ban was placed on arms to Spain. Roosevelt, and also Claude Bowers the US ambassador to Spain, were personally sympathetic to the Republic but the President was preoccupied with the Depression and with getting agreement on domestic, New Deal, legislation. He, like the British government, wished to contain the conflict. In addition, he had to consider the sharp differences of opinion within the United States, where liberal and intellectual support for the Republic conflicted with Catholic support for the Nationalists. Meantime, the US Texas Oil company supplied the Nationalists with oil on credit. 'The business of America,' as a previous President had said, 'is business'.

Non-intervention did not at all impede German and Italian aid to the Nationalists and it had the unintended effect of making the Republic almost wholly dependent on the Soviet Union, which in turn promoted Soviet influence in Republican Spain.

8 The Impact of Foreign Involvement

a) On the course of the war

The Nationalists certainly received more aid than the Republic. Exact estimates are difficult to make since military aid was concealed, but it is calculated that German assistance to the Nationalists amounted to about 10,000 military personnel, 600-800 aircraft and 200 tanks. Italian aid comprised approximately 60,000 troops, 600-750 aircraft and 150 tanks. Soviet aid to the Republic consisted of a few hundred military advisors, 800-1,000 aircraft and 500-730 tanks, while the French sent about 150 aircraft in the first weeks of the war. The Republic also had the 35,000 men in the International Brigades.

The timing and quality of aid was, however, more important than the quantity. For example, the Nationalists benefited significantly from the airlift of the Moroccan army, while Soviet tanks and planes (which were faster and superior to the German/Italian models at that time) were vital in saving Madrid in November and December 1936. However, by the time of the 1938 offensives, Soviet aid was diminishing. Also, although the Soviet aircraft were superior to the German models in 1936, by 1937 and 1938 this was no longer the case as improved German fighters and bombers were introduced. As described in Chapter 6, it was the continuity, regularity and higher quality of the German/Italian aid which gave the Nationalists the edge, though this was not the only reason for their success.

b) On relations between the European powers

In retrospect, the western powers gained little from non-intervention. It did not lead to any real improvement in relations between Britain and Italy. In April 1938 an Anglo-Italian agreement was signed which provided for Italian troops to be withdrawn from Spain, preservation of the status quo in the Mediterranean and British recognition of Italian conquests in Abyssinia. But by this time joint intervention in the war had already served to bring Germany and Italy much closer together. In October 1936 the two powers had signed the Rome-Berlin Axis and in 1937 Italy joined the Anti-Comintern Pact, and Mussolini conceded that Germany should be the dominant power in Austria. The process was completed with the May 1939 German-Italian Alliance, the Pact of Steel.

Soviet diplomacy in Spain also brought few benefits to Stalin, who by the end of 1938 had to contemplate not only the imminent defeat of the Republic but also his failure to achieve any concrete agreements with the western powers. British-French appeasement of Germany at the Munich Conference in September 1938, to which he was not invited, helped lead Stalin to the view that a Soviet pact with Germany might be the best short-term method of avoiding war.

Italy too achieved little in practical terms. Its army in Spain had performed disappointingly, the war was expensive and none of Mussolini's Mediterranean ambitions was achieved.

The power that gained most from intervention was Germany. Hitler acquired a possible ally in Franco, weakened France and forged an alliance with Italy which made *Anschluss* (union) with Austria possible. Moreover, the prolonged conflict in Spain had served to distract the western powers from the German plans to take over Austria and Czechoslovakia in 1938. Hitler, therefore, of all the statesmen involved in Spain, had the best reason to be satisfied with the results of his policy.

References

1   *Documents on German Foreign Policy 1918-45*, Series D, Vol 1 (HMSO, 1949), pp.171-72.
2   M. Muggeridge (ed), *Ciano's Diplomatic Papers* (Odhams, 1948), p.144
3   Hugh Thomas, *The Spanish Civil War* (Penguin, 1986), p. 389
4   Quoted in A. Adamthwaite, *The Lost Peace, International Relations in Europe, 1918-1939* (Edward Arnold, 1980), pp.175-77
5   Quoted in A. Adamthwaite, *The Making of the Second World War* (Allen & Unwin, 1977), pp.160-61.
6   Thomas, *Spanish Civil War*, p.344.
7   Anthony Eden, *The Eden Memoirs, Facing the Dictators* (Cassell, 1962), p.406.
8   Quoted in *Spanish Front, writers on the Civil War* (Oxford University Press, 1986), p.32.
9   Jason Gurney, *Crusade in Spain* (Faber, 1974), p.76.
10 Quoted in G. Esenwein & A. Shubert, *Spain at War, The Spanish Civil War in context 1931-1939* (Longman, 1995), p.192.
11 Thomas, *The Spanish Civil War*, p.744.

Summary Diagram
Foreign Powers and the War

Intervention

Aid to the Republic	Aid to the Nationalists

Pro-Soviet government in Spain
Soviet Union

Security against Germany | Good relations with UK and France

Tanks, aircraft, military advisers

International Brigades

35,000 mainly from France and other European countries

Established pro-German government
Germany

Anti-commu-nism | Weaken France

Economic benefits

Airlift of Moroccan Army
Condor Legion, aircraft, tanks

Mediterranean empire
Italy

Anti-communism | Weaken France

Influence in Spain | Prestige following Abyssinia

Airlift of Moroccan Army
60,000 troops

Non-intervention

Britain	USA	France
Prevent war spreading Appease Italy Anti-communism Gibraltar Economic interests	Isolationism Depression and New Deal	Political divisions within France. Influence of UK govern-ment. Prevent war spreading

Non-intervention Committee

Ineffective in preventing intervention

 The results of intervention ◄

In Spain

Nationalists benefited more due to quantity, quality and timing of aid

For the European powers

Germany: gained most in terms of strategic position and Italian friendship
Italy: few tangible benefits
USSR: no benefits - failed to keep Republic in power and alienated Britain and France
Britain and France: few benefits

Source-based questions on 'Foreign Powers and the War'

Read the four extracts on pages 68 and 69, which give different views of Blum's decision not to aid the Republic and on the role of the British Government in his decision. Answer the following questions:

a) Explain the phrase 'breakage of the political unity of Western Europe' (page 68, lines 6-7). (2 marks)

b) Why would the Pyrenees frontier, the Balearic Isles, the Straits of Gibraltar and the Canaries (page 68, line 6) be expected to be of importance to the French Government? (4 marks)

c) What reasons are given in extract 1 to explain Blum's decision to refuse aid to Spain? (5 marks)

d) To what extent do the accounts given in extracts 3 and 4 disagree with each other? (3 marks)

e) Why, in retrospect, might Blum wish to place some responsibility on Britain for his decision not to aid the Republic, and why might Eden wish to disclaim this? (4 marks)

f) To what extent and for what reasons might historians regard extracts 1 and 2 as valuable evidence for the French Government's motives in refusing aid to Spain? (7 marks)

6 The Military Events of the War from September 1936 to March 1939

The war divides into three main phases. The first, from September 1936 to March 1937, was dominated by the Nationalist attempt to take Madrid. The second, by the Nationalist attack on the Republican zone in northern Spain, which was conquered by October 1937. The third and last part of the war began with the Nationalist offensive in central Spain in February 1938 and ended with their victory in March 1939.

At what point did it become clear that the Republic would lose? Some historians consider that it faced so many political and military problems that it was effectively doomed from the start and was fortunate to survive as long as it did. But we saw in Chapter 3 that, although the Nationalists made some significant gains in the weeks following the rising, the two sides were still fairly evenly matched in the Autumn of 1936. This was still the case in March 1937 when the Nationalists had failed to take Madrid despite their best efforts. Not till the Summer of 1937 did it begin to appear that the Republic might lose. The first major turning point in the war was the Nationalist conquest of northern Spain between March and October 1937, which was a great blow to the Republic, reducing both its territory and industrial resources. The second turning point was the successful Nationalist offensive in the Spring of 1938 which reached the Mediterranean, cutting the remaining Republican territory in half. This made it certain that Franco would eventually be the victor, though the Republic struggled on for several more months.

1 Military Organisation

Apart from the Moroccan campaigns, the Spanish army had not fought a war for many years, and both sides faced shortages of modern armaments (and sometimes even of reliable maps). Rifles, grenades and machine guns were often obsolete leftovers from earlier wars and frequently failed to work. Both sides were dependent on foreign aid.

The Republic, however, not only experienced more military problems than the Nationalists but found it harder to resolve them. In the first few crucial weeks of the war, the government had neither an organised army nor central control of military operations. The various fronts in Madrid, Aragon, northern and southern Spain, all operated semi-independently and the Republic was trying to fight a series of local wars rather than one concerted campaign.

In July 1936, with the army in disarray, the immediate defence of the Republic rested on hastily-formed militias, together with sections of the Assault guard and the Civil Guard. Though approximately half the officers in the regular army had not joined the rebellion they were not trusted by the Government since they were suspected of being secretly pro-Nationalist and therefore unreliable. Of the 7,300 officers in the Republican zone, only half were eventually classified as loyal.

Meanwhile, the anarchist and POUM militias refused to recognise military ranks, elected their officers, wanted debates and votes on all issues and competed with one another for scarce supplies and equipment. The photograph below shows members of the Anarchist militias on the Aragon front in 1936. Note that they are dressed in ordinary clothes, rather than uniforms, and their casual demeanour makes them look very different from regular soldiers. The militias were enthusiastic but ill-disciplined. The following account of a Republican officer's encounter with some militiamen on the Aragon front in August 1936 illustrates some of the problems they presented:

1   On approaching Sarinena I came across a truck halted on the other side of the highway, and at the request of a group of soldiers stopped my car. Their truck had broken down but they did not know what was wrong with it ...

5   'Where are you going?' I asked them with surprise.
     'To Barcelona to spend the Sunday there.'
     'But aren't you supposed to be at the front?'
     'Sure, but as there's nothing doing we are going to Barcelona.'
     'Have you been given leave?'
10   'No. Can't you see we are militiamen?'

Militiamen

In October 1936 Largo Caballero, who was War Minister as well as Prime Minister, began to replace the militias with a regular army, the prototype for which was the Communist Party's Fifth Regiment. Conscription was introduced and the army was organised in so-called 'mixed' brigades of combined infantry and tanks. Traditional army organisation was followed in most respects, except for the introduction of Soviet style political commissars whose role was to reinforce the political aspects of the struggle and raise morale. Historians generally agree that this Popular Army proved to be more efficient than the militias. They argue that the Nationalist army could only be countered by an equally conventional and disciplined force. But the new army, though supported by the Communists and most of the Socialists, was unpopular with non-communist left wing-groups and the militias resisted incorporation into it.

The Nationalists at first faced a similar situation with numerous semi-independent 'columns' of Carlist and Falangist militias operating alongside regular army units. However, they were able to restructure their army more quickly and easily than the Republicans. They were helped by the fact that Generals, not politicians, controlled military operations and Franco's combined roles of Head of State and Commander in Chief avoided the conflicts and tensions which beset the Republic. Another advantage was that the Nationalist part of the army continued to function normally following the rebellion and the loyalty of the officers was taken as read. A high proportion of younger junior officers had joined the rebellion and the Nationalists (unlike the Republic) also succeeded in training additional numbers of such officers during the war. They had also, in the Army of Africa, the best trained and equipped portion of the whole Spanish Army. The Moorish troops were particularly adept at concealment and rapid movement in open country, which was a great asset in the advance from Seville to Madrid. And, by early 1937, the Carlists and the Falange militias had been absorbed into the regular army.

Another difference between the two sides lay in the degree of foreign control over strategy and tactics. Republican military strategy came to be increasingly dominated by Soviet advisors. This led to conflicts with those politicians and officers who either disliked the Communists or resented foreign interference. Also, Republican commanders were a heterogeneous mixture of regular army officers, Spanish communists (sometimes trained in the USSR), such as Lister and Modesto, and foreign born Communists, and these groups often conflicted. The Nationalist commanders, on the other hand, were all Spanish career officers who shared a similar training and outlook.

2 The Battle for Madrid, October 1936 to March 1937

Madrid the capital city, was the Nationalists' first objective. From July to September 1936 Franco's forces rapidly advanced northwards to link up with Mola's troops and it was quite possible that the city might have been captured by October (see the map of Spain in March 1937 on page 82). But the attack was delayed when Franco decided to divert part of his army to relieve the Alcázar (fortress) in Toledo, which was being besieged by the Republicans. In the Alcázar, a small force of Nationalists under Colonel Moscardó had been holding out in increasingly desperate conditions since July. From a purely military point of view Toledo could easily have been bypassed but it had great symbolic significance and the Nationalist defence had acquired an epic stature.

Franco's motives were probably partly political, since the prestige gained from raising the siege on 27 September assisted him in consolidating his position as Head of State. But the Alcázar episode was also an early example of his general strategy, which was to retake every piece of territory lost, even if militarily unimportant. These tactics were frequently the despair of his German and Italian advisors, who were exasperated at what they regarded as the slow, ponderous progress of the Nationalist armies. Franco's strategy was due to a desire to conserve resources and to thoroughly subdue each piece of territory taken, so that, as he put it to the Italian Ambassador in April 1937, 'there will be less glory but more internal peace afterwards.' [2] They may also have resulted from a wish to prolong the war until his political position was unassailable

The Toledo detour possibly cost the Nationalists their chance to capture Madrid, since by the time they turned their attention to the capital, the Republic had had time to improvise a defence, and the first Soviet aid - 50 tanks and 100 aircraft - together with the International Brigades, had arrived in Spain. However, the Nationalist command was still confident that the city would fall and its position at the end of October seemed hopeless. This view was shared by Largo Caballero, who, on 6 November decided to move the government to Valencia, leaving General Miaja in charge of the defence. Against all the odds, Miaja rose to the occasion and established a Defence Council of representatives of all the political parties. His successful generalship soon made him a popular hero in the Republic, though his second-in-command, Rojo, was responsible for many of the detailed tactical decisions.

On 1 November Nationalist troops under Varela had reached the suburbs of Madrid and on 4 November captured the airport. November 8 and 9 were the crucial days when the main Nationalist offensive, assisted by German and Italian tanks, was launched from the west through an area of open scrubland, the Casa del Campo, and

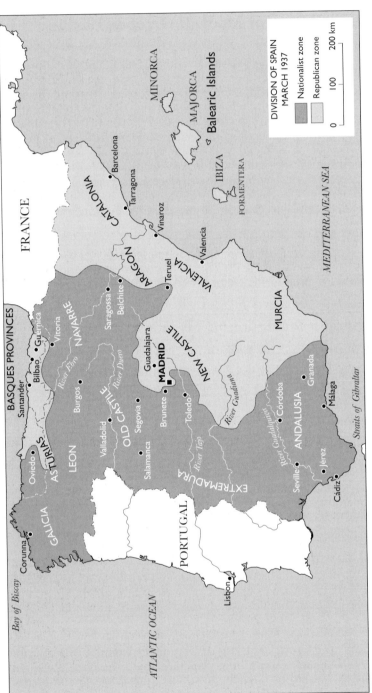

Spain in March 1937

across the River Manzanares towards the centre of the city. Amazingly, the Republican forces held off this attack. By 16 November the fighting had shifted to the University in the north-west of the city where anarchists and members of the International Brigades were engaged in desperate hand-to-hand fighting among the buildings with the Moors of the Foreign Legion. As a member of the International Brigades described it, 'sometimes we would be holding the top floors and sniping from the roofs, while Moors were holding the lower floors; sometimes it was the other way round.'[3] Though the Nationalists established themselves in parts of the University, their advance petered out, and from 23 November, when it was clear that Madrid was not going to fall immediately, direct attacks were halted.

The successful defence of Madrid has been variously credited either to the International Brigades or to the mobilisation of thousands of the ordinary inhabitants of the city assisted by the arrival of a 4,000 strong anarchist column under Durruti (who was to be killed in the battle). The appearance of the International Brigades did greatly improve morale, which had been damaged by the flight of the government. But it is now generally considered that they were too few in number and too inexperienced to have been the determining factor. Raymond Carr considers that their role has been exaggerated and 'it was the remaining units of the old army and security forces and … the new "Mixed Brigades" commanded by professional officers who were loyal to the Republic, which saved Madrid.'[4]

Many civilians certainly took part in the fighting, and there was a mood of determination and defiance, exemplified in such slogans as: 'No pasaran!' (they will not pass) and 'Madrid will be the tomb of fascism'. But equally, if not more, important than popular participation was Republican air superiority. The Soviet planes (Moscas and Chatos) were superior to the German and Italian models at this point in the war. Another reason for the successful Republican defence was their advantage in numbers - they had an estimated 23,000 men as against the Nationalists' 8,000. Franco's forces were relatively small since he was unwilling to risk his reserves and had problems with supplies and long lines of communication. The Moroccan troops were less successful in street fighting than they had been in open country. The Republic, in any case, usually performed better in defence than in attack. Lastly, Miaja benefited from the fortuitous capture of the Nationalist plans just before the start of the battle.

From December 1936, Madrid settled down to a long siege punctuated by frightening air raids. It is possible that had the Republic immediately counter-attacked at this point they might have gained the advantage, but their troops were too exhausted for this to be a practical possibility. Instead, the initiative remained with the Nationalists, who were boosted by the arrival of the German Condor Legion and by Italian troops.

Franco was still intent on capturing Madrid and now adopted

indirect tactics, trying to encircle the city and cut its communications with the rest of Republican territory. This was first attempted in December, when the Nationalists attacked the Corunna road to the north-west of Madrid. Fighting centred on the town of Boadilla but they got no further towards their objective.

The next move came in February 1937 when General Orgaz attacked from the south-west across the River Jarama, aiming to cut the Madrid-Valencia road which was the main route for essential supplies to the capital. The Moors and Foreign Legion, backed by German tanks, crossed the river and engaged in fierce fighting with the International Brigades with heavy casualties on both sides. But again, largely thanks to Soviet aircraft and tanks, the Nationalists were halted well short of their objective, gaining only a few miles of territory.

Finally, in March 1937 a further attack occurred, this time to the north east of Madrid, at Guadalajara (see the map on page 82). When it was clear that little progress was being made at Jarama, Franco reluctantly agreed that Italian troops under General Roatta should play the more important role in the next attack. Their offensive, however, completely failed. In extremely cold, wet weather the Italian tanks and trucks were stranded in mud, their planes were grounded and they were pushed back. Soviet tanks proved on this occasion superior to the Italian variety. Franco did not welcome the prospect of Italian troops being more successful than Spaniards, and it is possible that he may therefore have deliberately delayed in sending reinforcements. The Italian humiliation at Guadalajara gave him a welcome opportunity to disperse Italian troops in Spanish units, thereby subordinating them to Spanish commanders.

The battle of Jarama ended in a draw and Guadalajara counted as a moral victory for the Republicans, though they had only gained a few square miles of territory. Meanwhile, the Nationalists in southern Spain under Queipo de Llano had been more successful, capturing in February 1937 the coastal town of Málaga, which was inadequately defended by militias.

By March 1937 Franco faced an impasse in Madrid. He therefore made an important decision to change his strategy and temporarily abandoned the attack on the capital in order to concentrate most of his forces on the capture of northern Spain. This region was the weakest point of the Republic, cut off as it was from the remainder of their zone, and it offered the prospect of quick and easy success with substantial rewards.

3 The War in the North, March to October 1937

In northern Spain the Republicans were at a serious disadvantage (see the map on page 82). They were cut off from reinforcements and could not be supplied with tanks or planes except by sea, which was difficult, since the northern coast was blockaded by the Nationalist navy - the Republican navy remained largely inactive during the war due to lack of experienced officers. The north was also politically divided and the Basque state in the east, the central section around Santander, and the Asturias in the west were all governed separately. With their own language and cultural traditions, deeply religious and somewhat conservative, the Basques were an anomaly in the Republic, which they supported mainly because it had granted them some self-government. Their state of Euzkadi was fiercely independent and resisted all attempts by the government in Valencia to establish an overall military command over the area. Llano de Encomienda was appointed commander for the whole northern front, but his authority was disregarded by the Basques. There was thus no co-ordinated strategy to resist the Nationalist attack.

In April 1937, the Nationalists under Mola moved into Basque territory. The most dramatic episode of the early stages of the campaign was the destruction on 26 April of the Basque town of Guernica by the Condor Legion. For three hours the town was bombed with explosive bombs and incendiaries and the inhabitants machine-gunned. As it was a market day the town was crowded and, of the 7,000 population, 1,685 were killed and 900 injured. Guernica had some strategic importance since it had an arms plant and was on a major route to the north, but in fact the military targets were left intact. One possible motive for the attack may well have been to demoralise the Basques, since the town was their capital and the Guernica tree was the symbol of Basque nationalism. Also, the fate of Guernica could be relied on to inspire terror in the inhabitants of Bilbao and other northern cities.

Guernica was one of the first examples of terror bombing of civilians and as such was widely publicised and condemned. It is commemorated in Picasso's famous painting of the same name. At the time and for many years afterwards, Franco's government denied all responsibility and blamed the Basque militias for the destruction, but this version was never generally believed. Instead, debate centred on the relative responsibility of the Germans and the Nationalist government. Till recently, many historians believed that Guernica was a Condor Legion initiative, possibly undertaken because the Germans were impatient with the slow Spanish/Italian advance. Paul Preston however, considers that recent evidence points to its destruction being ordered by the Nationalists,[5] though it is not clear whether Franco personally knew about it in advance.

The following sources provide different interpretations of the destruction of Guernica. The first is an eyewitness account by a Basque priest:

I I arrived in Guernica on April 26th at 4.40 pm. I had hardly left the car when the bombardment began. The people were terrified. They fled

abandoning their livestock in the market place. The bombardment lasted until 7.45. During that time five minutes did not elapse without the skies
5 being black with German planes. The planes descended very low, the machine gun fire tearing up the woods and roads, in whose gutters huddled together, lay old men, women and children. Before long it was impossible to see as far as 500 yards owing to the heavy smoke. Fire enveloped the whole city ... As a Catholic priest I state that no worse
10 outrage could be inflicted on religion than the Te Deum to be sung to the glory of Franco in the church at Guernica which was miraculously saved by the heroism of the firemen from Bilbao. [6]

The next extract is an account by a British journalist who arrived in Guernica on the night of 26 April:

1 Guernica, the most ancient town of the Basques and the centre of their cultural tradition, was completely destroyed yesterday afternoon by insurgent raiders. The bombardment of this open town far behind the lines occupied precisely three hours and a quarter, during which a
5 powerful fleet of aeroplanes ... did not cease in unloading on the town bombs weighing from 1000lb downwards ... The fighters meanwhile plunged low from above ... to machine gun those of the civilian population who had taken refuge in the fields. [7]

A completely different version is given in this account by Luis Bolín, a leading Nationalist:

1 During the advance on Bilbao, Guernica became part of the front line. It contained several small factories, one of them engaged in the manufacture of arms and ammunition. It was an important road junction ... and a depot of substantial size for the massing of reserves on their way
5 to the trenches ... The Republicans in Bilbao needed a sensational story to offset their reverses. They dispatched Asturian miners to dynamite Guernica and set fire to its buildings and swore that they had been blown to smithereens by German bombs ... To destroy an entire small town ... not hundreds but thousands of bombs would be required. The
10 resources for such wholesale destruction are entirely lacking to either side in this war ... It should be noted that the destruction though involving many buildings spared the Guernica tree and adjoining structure. Basque separatists took great care not to damage the tree which they held in special veneration. [8]

From Guernica the Nationalists pressed on towards Bilbao. The Basques had built a defence, the so-called 'ring of iron', around this town but it was inadequately constructed, and furthermore the Nationalists had acquired the plans. Bilbao was captured in June 1937, amid scenes of panic when many of the population tried unsuccessfully to escape by sea. Instead of contributing to the defence of the remainder of the north, the Basque armies melted away. The Nationalists moved on to capture Santander in August, Gijón in

September and rest of the Asturias by October 1937.

In the northern campaign the numbers of troops on each side were roughly equal but the Nationalists had the advantage of many more tanks and aircraft, since the Republican air force based in central Spain did not have sufficient range to participate. The campaign was a turning point in the war, as a result of which Franco made vital gains. More territory was captured and the Nationalists by Autumn 1937 controlled about two-thirds of Spain. The Republic lost about 25 per cent of its armed forces. The Nationalists gained valuable resources of coal and iron, as well as armaments industries, and a population which could be used as forced labour or conscripted into the army, giving them an estimated extra 65,000 troops to fight in the centre and south. The Nationalist navy was also freed from the northern blockade to concentrate on disrupting Republican supply routes in the Mediterranean.

4 Republican Offensives, June to December 1937

While the Nationalists were advancing in the north the Republic could only win back the initiative by mounting a successful campaign of its own. A Republican breakthrough would at the very least oblige the Nationalists to send reinforcements and would slow down their conquest of the north. But until July 1937 little was done. In May, Largo Caballero had proposed an advance south-west of Madrid to Mérida on the Portuguese frontier. This was a risky plan but, had it succeeded, it would have split the Nationalist zone in two and transformed the military situation. However, it was opposed by Miaja, Rojo and the Communists in the political infighting which preceded Largo's removal from power, and rejected in favour of a less ambitious version, which was to break through the Nationalist front at one of its weakest points at Brunete west of Madrid and encircle the Nationalists besieging the city.

The Brunete offensive, planned by Rojo, began on 6 July 1937. The Republicans had 80,000 men and a large contingent of tanks, and the surprise attack was at first successful. But after a few days it ground to a halt gaining only a few miles of territory at the expense of heavy casualties. In the fighting in the hot summer weather the Republic lost 25,000 men and the Nationalists 17,000.

In August 1937 the Republicans again tried to break through the Nationalist lines, this time on the Aragon front, with the objective of capturing the town of Belchite and, ultimately, Saragossa. After initial success, this attack, like Brunete, slowed down and was soon driven back by a counter-attack backed by superior aircraft and artillery.

Finally, in December 1937, an offensive with the now fully reorganised Popular Army was launched in central Spain, against Teruel, a provincial capital which was already almost surrounded by

Troops at Teruel

Republican troops. It was designed to relieve the pressure on Madrid where, following his conquest of the north, Franco had again turned his attention. This time it seemed the Republicans would be more successful. Freezing temperatures meant that the Nationalists could not use their planes or tanks and Teruel fell in January 1938. The photograph above shows the battle-weary Republican soldiers near Teruel and some of the destruction resulting from the battle. However, events at Teruel soon followed the previous pattern when Nationalists counter-attacked and re-captured the town in February. Henceforth the Republic was on the defensive as Franco massed his troops for an advance to the Mediterranean.

The inability of the Republic to sustain these offensives was critical to the outcome of the war. There are several reasons for their failure. 1937 saw the first appearance of German Messerschmidt 109 fighters, which were faster than the Russian models and enabled the Nationalists to achieve air superiority. At Brunete, the Nationalists used their tanks to better advantage in concentrated formations. In addition, the Republican campaigns were dogged by political disputes and bitter personal recriminations, for example between the commanders at Teruel, where El Campesino (the peasant) accused the communists Lister and Modesto of deliberately orchestrating his defeat for party-political reasons.

Equally important was the Nationalists' ability to successfully defend their positions until reinforcements arrived. This owed much to the training and skills of their junior officers - the rank on whom, in the confusion of battle, success or failure often depended - and to their superior communications systems.

The Republic's failures in 1937 greatly reduced its chances of winning the war, condemning it, at best, to a defensive strategy.

5 Nationalist Victory: the War from January 1938 to March 1939

Franco had insisted on re-taking Teruel against the advice of the Germans and Italians who wanted him to concentrate on Madrid. But the re-capture of the town provided him with a unique opportunity to achieve the breakthrough which was to win the war. By the beginning of 1938 the Nationalist Army already numbered 600,000, a third larger than the Republican army. From Teruel they maintained their impetus and advanced rapidly into Republican territory meeting little resistance. In April 1938 they reached the sea at Vinaroz, separating Catalonia from Valencia, thereby cutting the remaining Republican zone in two (see the map of Spain in July 1938 on page 90.

The plight of the Republic was now desperate and Negrín, the Prime Minister, had little option but to try to hang on as long as possible against the increasing odds. His only real chance was an outbreak of a general European war which might lead the Western democracies to aid the Republic or force the Nationalists to make a compromise peace. In the Spring and Summer of 1938 such a European war seemed a possibility. Hitler's foreign policy had grown more aggressive and in March 1938 he absorbed Austria into Germany and began threatening Czechoslovakia. The Republic also obtained a respite, when Franco decided to move against Valencia rather than Catalonia, which would have been an easier target. This decision was due to fear of French intervention should the fighting approach their frontier.

Valencia did indeed prove difficult to conquer and, in the Summer of 1938, the Nationalists were held up by stiff resistance. At this point,

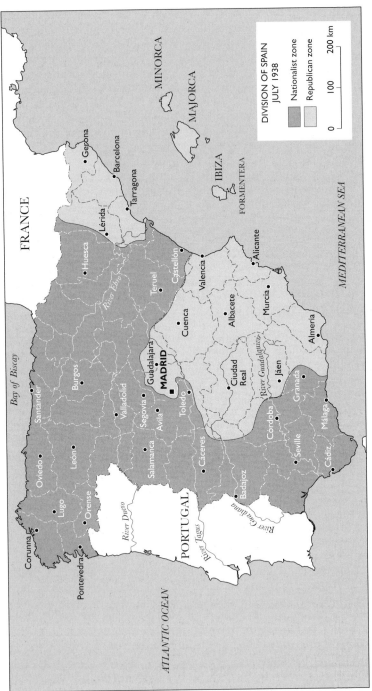

DIVISION OF SPAIN
JULY 1938

Nationalist zone
Republican zone

0   100   200 km

FRANCE

MINORCA

MAJORCA

Gerona
Barcelona
Tarragona

Lérida

IBIZA
FORMENTERA

MEDITERRANEAN SEA

Huesca

Teruel

Castellón

Valencia

Alicante

River Ebro

Cuenca

Albacete

Murcia

Almería

Bay of Biscay

Santander

Burgos

Guadalajara
MADRID
Toledo

Ciudad
Real

Jaén

River Guadalquivir

Granada

Oviedo

León

Valladolid

Segovia
Ávila

Salamanca

Córdoba

Seville

Málaga

Lugo

Orense

Cáceres

Badajoz

Cádiz

Corunna

Pontevedra

River Duero

PORTUGAL

River Tagus

River Guadiana

ATLANTIC OCEAN

Spain in 1938

the Republic put all its efforts into a last counter-offensive. On the night of 24/25 July thousands of Popular Army troops successfully crossed the River Ebro at Gandesa using pontoons and inflatable rubber boats, and engaged the Nationalists in the mountainous areas beyond. The Ebro campaign was a great achievement, given the Republic's limited resources, and fighting continued throughout the Summer, but by November its troops were once more in retreat. This was effectively the end, for the Republic was now totally exhausted, and its final defeat was only a matter of time.

In the 1938 campaigns the Nationalists' main advantage was their domination of the air. The new German Messerschmidts and Heinkels and Italian Savoias were all faster, lighter and had greater fire power than the Soviet aircraft. Also by 1938, Soviet aid to the Republic was reduced as Stalin became pessimistic about success in Spain. The remaining members of the International Brigades were withdrawn in October 1938 and given an emotional send-off in Barcelona. Any hope of assistance from the Western democracies also evaporated. At Munich in September 1938, Hitler was awarded the Sudetenland in Czechoslovakia and a European war was averted. In the cartoon on page 92, the British Prime Minister, Chamberlain, is portrayed as appeasing Hitler at Munich and, in the process, sacrificing Spain as well. Note that the cartoonist implies that Spain was being handed over to Mussolini, which did not turn out to be the case.

Having pushed the Republicans back over the Ebro, Franco advanced rapidly into Catalonia, taking Barcelona in February 1939. A stream of refugees flooded over the frontier into France. In February 1939 Britain and France finally recognised Franco's government.

The fall of Barcelona left only south-central Spain, from Madrid to Valencia, in the hands of the Republic. Here Miaja still commanded a substantial army. But there was little prospect of its being used since in the final days of the war fighting broke out among the Republicans themselves. Negrín and the Communist members of the government favoured continuing the war despite the overwhelming odds, but they were in a minority. By this time, Negrín was reduced to being a 'politician without a party as well as a war leader without an army'.[9] In opposition to Negrín, Colonel Casado on 5 March 1939 headed a coup of army officers in Madrid - a final *pronunciamiento* - and with the support of the anarchists set up a rival government, the National Defence Council. Fighting broke out in Madrid between Casado's supporters and the Communists. Casado won, but this benefited him little, since his expectation that he would be able to negotiate reasonable terms with Franco was unrealistic. The latter continued to insist on unconditional surrender and Casado had no alternative but to comply. The few days of negotiations did, however, gain time for most Republican leaders, including Negrín, to escape into exile abroad.

On 28 March the Nationalists finally occupied Madrid, in spite of its importance the last city to fall to them, and on 31 March the war was officially over. It had lasted much longer than expected, 2 years and 8 months, and ended, fortunately for Franco, just a few months before the outbreak of the Second World War.

EUROPE'S AUCTIONEER
"——And, of course, this one for you, Sir."

Chamberlain appeases Hitler at the Munich Conference

6 The Costs of the War

These were immense both in terms of casualties and damage to the economy. Of the Spanish population of about 25 million, it is estimated that 175,000 Republicans and 110,000 Nationalists were killed in action and many more than that number wounded. This was in addition to the estimated 130,000 or more civilians killed by both sides and the 25,000 victims of the Nationalist air raids. It is thought that up to 220,000 Spaniards also died due to starvation, malnutrition or disease attributable to the war. Over 400,000 Republicans had fled from Spain into exile and there were still about 200,000 Republican supporters in Franco's prisons in July 1939.

The war also left Spain economically ravaged. Railways, roads and bridges had been destroyed and industry and agriculture depleted. Food shortages were a serious problem; there was a huge black market in food and consumer goods and rampant corruption. The 'Hungry Years', as they were called, lasted until the mid 1950s.

7 Why did the Nationalists Win the War ?

It is generally agreed that the Nationalists owed their success to a combination of four inter-related reasons: foreign intervention, military organisation and tactics, economic and financial factors and the internal politics of Republican and Francoist Spain. Where historians disagree is about the relative importance of these reasons.

Nationalist success is often attributed to the greater military aid received by the Nationalists from Germany and Italy, and conversely to the betrayal of the Republic by Britain and France - a war determined 'in the chancelleries of Europe rather than on the battlefields of Spain.'[10] Earlier histories often assumed this to be the only reason for the outcome and it is still considered to be important. But on its own this explanation is inadequate. Foreign aid was certainly important and, as described in Chapter 5, the Nationalists received more, both quantitatively and qualitatively. Their allies provided aid consistently up to the end of the war, and on easier terms than did the Soviet Union. But there were times, for example the Autumn of 1936, when Soviet assistance gave the Republic the advantage, and other occasions, for instance in the 1937 offensives, when the two sides were more evenly matched.

Until recently underestimated, but arguably as important as military aid, were the financial and economic advantages which the Nationalists possessed. Most of the international business community favoured them and made it easy for them to obtain the credit essential to purchase war supplies, while putting obstacles in the way of the Republic. The Republican defeat can be partly attributed to the economic embargo operated by Britain, France and the USA. It has been estimated that the Nationalists received at least 700 million dollars worth of goods and services on credit during the war.[11] In the Summer of 1936, for example, the Majorcan millionaire Juan March provided about £1 million for the purchase of Italian bombers. In spite of official US neutrality, Franco was supplied throughout the war with oil and other vital commodities by American companies such as Texaco, Texas Oil Company and Firestone Rubber.

The Nationalists also controlled the food-producing regions of Spain and were able to export wheat and other agricultural products in return for foreign exchange. In contrast, the Republic had little to trade with and lacked the raw materials to keep its industries working. It has been estimated that by the end of the war Catalonia was producing only one-third of its 1936 output. The loss of the industrial resources in northern Spain was a great blow and the Republic ended up by being almost totally dependent on the Soviet Union.

In the last resort, though, success or failure depended on the performance of the respective armies, which, despite the emphasis in propaganda on International Brigades and Italian 'volunteers', consisted largely of Spaniards. Both sides made mistakes in military strategy, but the Republic made more, and missed vital opportunities - for example to prevent the Nationalist advance in the opening weeks of the war, or to break through the Nationalist lines in 1937. The Republic suffered from its inability to organise as effective an army as the Nationalists or to establish central control over the variety of local fronts till too late. Michael Alpert considers that the clash between the anarchist and communist concepts of an army, led to the worst of both worlds: 'over-authoritarian and bureaucratic organisation combined with frequent examples of poor discipline.'[12]

As seen in section 4 of this chapter, the Republic's most serious deficiency was its inability to sustain the momentum of any of its major offensives, though these were often well-planned on paper. There was little that could be done to prevent Franco's advance in northern Spain in 1937, but success at Brunete, Belchite or Teruel might have countered this. This failure was mostly due to the inexperience and lack of training of junior officers, failures in communications systems, and political quarrels - all areas where the Nationalists had the advantage. It has been argued that, in view of the hostility of much of the population to the Nationalists, militia guerrilla tactics behind the enemy lines might have proved more effective than conventional warfare. However, though these might have prolonged the fighting they would have been unlikely to have won the war.

Military factors cannot be disassociated from political developments in the two zones. Here again the Nationalists held the advantage, acquiring a much greater degree of political unity and cohesion than the Republicans (see Chapter 7). Franco also discouraged too much German or Italian influence in Spanish affairs. In contrast (as seen in Chapter 4), Republican political conflict continued throughout the war and Soviet influence increased. Paul Heywood considers these political divisions to have been a key factor in accounting for the success of the Nationalists. 'The Republic was at war ... with much of the world. Most importantly and tragically, however, they were often at war with themselves.'[13]

In the hierarchy of causes of Republican defeat a combination of various military and political reasons can be identified as the most important, but exactly where the balance lies will be continue to be debated.

References

1   Quoted in Burnett Bolloten, *The Spanish Revolution* (University of North Carolina Press, 1979), pp.246-7.
2   Brian Crozier, *Franco* (Eyre & Spottiswoode, 1967), p.244.
3   Tom Wintringham, *English Captain* (Faber & Faber, 1939), p.137.
4   Raymond Carr, *The Spanish Tragedy* (Weidenfeld & Nicolson, 1977), p.156.
5   Paul Preston, *Franco* (Fontana Press, 1995), p.247.
6   Quoted in Paul Preston, *A concise history of the Spanish Civil War* (Fontana Press, 1996), p.193.

7   *The Times*, 28 April 1937.
8   Luis Bolin, *Spain, the vital years* (Cassell, 1967), pp.274-8.
9   Hugh Thomas, *The Spanish Civil War* (Penguin, 1986), p.905.
10 Preston, *A concise history of the Spanish Civil War*, p.99.
11 A. Vinas, 'The financing of the Spanish Civil War' in Paul Preston (ed),
    Revolution and War in Spain 1931-1939 (Methuen, 1984), p.281.
12 Michael Alpert, 'Uncivil War, the military struggle', in *History Today*,
    March 1989, p.19.
13 Paul Heywood, 'Why the Republic lost', in *History Today*, March 1989,
    p.27.

The Progress of the Nationalists from September 1936 to March 1939

Nationalist Failure		Nationalist Success
	Sept/Oct 1936	Advance of Army of Africa northwards
		Capture of Alcázar in Toledo
Failure to capture Madrid	Nov 1936	
	Feb 1937	
Battle of Guadalajara	March 1937	
	April 1937	Northern campaign
	June/July 1937	Failure of Republican offensives
	October 1937	Northern Spain occupied
Republicans seize Teruel	Jan 1938	
	Feb 1938	Recapture of Teruel and advance to Mediterranean
	April 1938	Mediterranean reached Republican zone split in two
Valencia difficult to conquer Republican Ebro offensive	July 1938	
	Nov 1938	Defeat of Ebro offensive
	Jan 1939	Capture of Catalonia
	March 1939	Madrid occupied End of War

Summary Diagram
The Military Events of the War from September 1936 to March 1939

Foreign Aid

Airlift from Morocco to mainland
German Condor Legion
Italian troops
Aid continued throughout the war
Few strings attached to aid
Air superiority by 1937/8

Military Organisation

Army of Africa
Unified military command
Militias soon absorbed into the army
Trained junior officers
Good communications
Successful offensives

Why did the Nationalists win the War?

Political factors

Franco Head of State and Commander in Chief
Falange and Carlists incorporated
Little foreign interference in internal affairs
Political unity

Financial/economic factors

International credit
Food producing areas
Industrial resources from 1937

Foreign aid

Soviet aid, but with political strings and reduced from 1938
Otherwise only International Brigades
Non-intervention in practice favoured the Nationalists

Military Organisation

Problems of militias
Independent fronts
Lack of trained junior officers
North cut off from rest of Republic
Failure of 1937 offensives
Political disputes

Why did the Republic lose the War?

Political factors

Political divisions throughout the war
Communists/Socialists versus anarchists and POUM
Soviet influence in government

Financial/economic factors

Lack of credit
Food shortages
Problems of collectives

Answering essay questions on why the Nationalists won the Civil War

Together with questions on the causes of the war, these are the most common types of essays set in examinations. To answer questions on the outcome of the war you would have to draw on material in Chapters 4, 5 and 7 as well as this chapter. Essay questions might ask why the Nationalists won or, conversely, why the Republic lost. In both cases the same material would be required, though with a different emphasis. Examples of questions are:

1. Discuss the view that the outcome of the Spanish Civil War owed little or nothing to the much publicised intervention of foreign powers.
2. Examine the view that the Republicans were defeated in the Spanish Civil War as much by their internal divisions as by the superior military resources of the enemy.

Some questions focus on the international involvement in the war for example:

3. Account for the international interest which was taken in the Spanish Civil War and for the savagery with which the war was fought.
4. Why were so many different countries interested in the Spanish Civil War, and why, despite this did the war not spread?

Other questions cover both the origins of the war and its outcome, as in:

5. Explain why democratic government proved so fragile in Spain between the two wars and why the Civil War resulted in victory for Franco.
6. When, during the 1930s, did it begin to seem that Spain could not avoid civil war and when, during the Civil War, did it begin to seem that the Republic would be defeated?

These questions would also draw on material from Chapters 2 and 3 and you would need to be careful to write much more concisely about each part. About half the answer should be on the causes of the war and half on the outcome.

Questions 1 and 2 can appear difficult because of the way in which they are worded. However, there are no absolutely right or wrong answers, though you must provide evidence for any arguments you put forward. Questions on the outcome of the war all require analysis and evaluation of the four main reasons for the Nationalist success (see the study diagram star chart, page 96). When planning the essay you should decide which factor(s) you think are the most important, in other words where the balance of the argument lies, and summarise these in the introduction.

At all costs avoid writing a narrative of the war! You should start with a list of reasons why the Nationalists won or the Republic lost, and use the events of the war as evidence: for example, Brunete and Belchite could be used as examples of the Republican failure to sustain offensives, and the Nationalists' superiority in air power from 1938 could be an example of the importance of foreign aid.

In planning such an essay it is useful to make a table of the advantages and disadvantages of each side in relation to the four main factors: foreign aid; military organisation; internal political divisions; and foreign credit and the economy. This would produce eight tables containing most of the information for the essay. One of these would be:

MILITARY ORGANISATION

Nationalist Advantages	Nationalist Disadvantages
The Army of Africa	Only half the Army at start of rebellion
Loyalty of officers	Semi-independent Carlist and Falange
Unified command	militias
Militias quickly merged into regular army	
Trained junior officers	
Good defensive tactics but also successful offensives	

The other seven tables would follow a similar pattern.

In question 4 it is relatively easy to summarise why Germany, Italy and the Soviet Union took an active role in the war and why Britain, France and even the USA were also concerned about it. What is more difficult is to assess why the war did not spread. This is partly because this part of the question requires some knowledge of European diplomacy in the 1930s. The main reason for the containment of the war is that none of the European powers wanted a major war, certainly not over Spain, at that time. Spain was a side-show as far as they were concerned. The powers which actively aided either side tried to disguise their intervention as far as possible. Britain and France were desperate to avoid a European war which they were not ready to fight, and Hitler and Mussolini were using Spain as a means to further more important ambitions.

Source based questions on the military events of the war

Read the three extracts on pages 85-6, which give different versions of the bombing of Guernica. Answer the following questions:

a) What indications are there in the content and language of extract 1 to suggest that the writer is an opponent of the Nationalists? (4 marks)

b) To what extent do the accounts in extracts 1 and 2 support one another? (4 marks)

c) How convincing are the arguments in extract 3 for the Asturian miners having destroyed Guernica? (4 marks)

d) Using the extracts and your own knowledge, explain why the Nationalists were so eager to deny that Guernica had been bombed by the Condor Legion. (5 marks)

e) Assess the value and limitations of all three extracts as evidence for the historian about the bombing of Guernica. (8 marks)

7 Nationalist Spain, July 1936 to March 1939 and beyond

At the start of the war the Nationalists were almost as politically divided as their opponents, but they resolved these problems much more successfully. Also, in Franco they acquired a leader who combined political and military power and whose authority increased as the war progressed.

1 Franco's Rise to Power, August to October 1936

Franco's rapid rise to prominence in Nationalist Spain was surprising since, among the conspirators, Generals Sanjurjo, Mola, and Goded were all initially more important. Nor was it clear in the early stages of the rebellion what form an eventual Nationalist government might take. But, given that the overriding priority was to win the war, the first Nationalist administration was a military junta set up in Burgos on 24 July by General Cabanellas. This Franco joined in early August.

Franco owed his success to a combination of luck and good management. He was fortunate in that most of his potential rivals either died or were discredited in the early stages of the war. Calvo Sotelo, the monarchist leader, had already been assassinated just prior to the Rising. General Sanjurjo was killed in a plane crash while on his way back to Spain from Portugal, and Goded was captured and executed after the collapse of the rebellion in Barcelona. José Antonio, the leader of the Falange, (see page 31) could have been a strong contender to Franco, but he was imprisoned by the Republicans in Spring 1936 and executed by them in November 1936; Franco discouraged attempts to get him released or rescued.

Mola was another possible contender for the leadership but his influence had declined. He had upset the Alfonsists because of his apparent preference for the Carlists and his refusal to let Don Juan, the Alfonsist heir to the throne, serve in the army, and they therefore transferred their loyalty to Franco in the crucial Autumn 1936 period. Gil Robles, the CEDA leader, was already discredited due to his party's failure to win seats in the February 1936 elections. He spent the first few months of the war in Lisbon and was cold-shouldered when he finally returned to Spain. Younger CEDA members were already flocking to join the Falange and the CEDA dissolved itself in February 1937.

However, luck is not the only explanation for Franco's rapid rise to power. The fact that the vital German and Italian aid was channelled exclusively through him also explains his success. Franco had made the most prompt and effective appeals for military assistance direct to Hitler, with well thought out requirements, while Mola on the other hand went through the official, but slower and more cautious, channels.

Further points in Franco's favour were his prestigious military career, his control of the Army of Africa, which was the most formidable section of the Nationalist army, and his rapid advance on Madrid in the Autumn of 1936. His campaigns in the first two months of the war, including the relief of the Alcázar, were also more spectacularly successful than those of the other commanders.

He was also paradoxically assisted by the fact that the rebellion was not an immediate success. If it had been, the most likely outcome would have been the restoration of the monarchy. But the longer the war went on, the more secure Franco's position became and the more remote a monarchical restoration.

All this left Franco a fairly clear field, provided he could persuade enough of the other generals to support him, and by September 1936 it was clear to most of them that the Nationalist armies needed a unified command if the war was to be won. Therefore, on 21 September, General Kindelán, the Chief of the Air Force and one of Franco's backers, organised a meeting at an airfield near Salamanca, where it was agreed that a commander in chief should be nominated to replace Sanjurjo. Franco was proposed by Generals Kindelán, Yagüe and Millán Astray, the commander of the Foreign Legion. Only Cabanellas opposed his nomination, though others, like Queipo de Llano, were unenthusiastic.

Franco now had overall military control, but he also wanted political power. On 28 September another meeting was arranged in Salamanca. By this time the relief of the Alcázar fortress in Toledo had further improved Franco's standing. With only Cabanellas against, a document was drafted which first designated him 'Head of State for the duration of the war', then 'Head of Government of the Spanish State' without a time limit. Franco was to further amend this wording in his favour by referring to himself simply as 'Head of State'. Cabanellas reluctantly signed the decree. The Generals' Junta of Defence was dissolved and replaced with an advisory body with Franco's brother Nicolás as secretary. The photograph on page 102 shows a self-satisfied Franco about to take office in Burgos on 1 October accompanied by Mola (on his right) and by some of the other Generals. The Nationalist headquarters were soon afterwards moved to Salamanca, where Franco took up residence in the Bishop's palace. He had now gone a long way to achieving his political objectives.

2 Franco's Relations with the Carlists and the Falange, September 1936 to April 1937

In order to fully secure his position Franco needed to neutralise both the Carlists and the Falange, either one of which might challenge his position. Both were mass movements by the Autumn of 1936. The Carlists possessed a large militia of more than 70,000 *requetés* who had played a significant part in the fighting in Navarre, while the Falange, the only genuine fascist party in Spain, had grown spectacularly since the rising with one million members by the beginning of 1937. The Falange militias comprised 19 per cent of all the Nationalist forces in October 1936. In tackling the problem posed by these two movements Franco owed much to the advice of his brother-in-law, Ramon Serrano Súñer, who escaped from the Republican zone in February 1937 and supplanted Nicolás Franco as his chief confidant. His great influence over the Generalissimo caused him to be nicknamed *cuñadísimo*, supreme brother-in-law.

Serrano Súñer was a more strategic thinker than Franco and set about convincing him of the necessity of filling the political power vacuum in Nationalist Spain. There were two options - a new Francoist party along the lines of that which had been attempted (unsuccessfully) by Primo de Rivera in the 1920s, or a fusion under Franco's control of the Carlists and the Falange. Súñer and Franco decided that the latter was the better prospect.

Franco had already gone some way towards weakening the Carlists.

General Franco walks to the Military Headquarters, accompanied by Generals Mola (on his left) and Cavakanti

In December 1936, with Mola's permission, their leader Fal Conde had tried to set up an independent military academy to train Carlist officers. The title of 'Royal Carlist Academy' was a deliberate provocation since it implied a possible restoration of the Carlist pretender. Franco reacted quickly and gave Fal Conde 48 hours to leave Spain or be court-martialled, following this up with a decree placing all the militias under army control. Fortunately for Franco, Rodezno, the other Carlist leader, proved more compliant and agreed to an eventual merger with the Falange.

The Falange was more formidable than the Carlists, though it was also the most appropriate vehicle for the new political movement envisaged by Serrano Súñer. Since July it had gained many new members. Some joined from defunct parties like the CEDA or out of opportunism - the so-called 'new shirts' to distinguish them from the original 'blue shirts'. Some were attracted by its ideology, which still included some radical ideas. The nickname FAIlange, (a reference to the anarchist FAI), implies that the Falange was seen by some as too left-wing, the Nationalist equivalent of the anarchists. The Falange benefited from the Nationalists' military dependence on Germany and Italy and it was initially backed by German and Italian representatives in Spain. It was, however, a party without an effective leader, a disadvantage which Franco was not slow to exploit. In September 1936, Manuel Hedilla, a provincial *jefe* (chief) and artisan from Santander, had been elected as a temporary leader until José Antonio should re-emerge. After the execution of José Antonio in November 1936, which some Falangists stubbornly refused to believe, the movement broke up into factions.

Franco had little ideological common ground with the Falange and no sympathy at all with its more radical ideas. But he seized the opportunity to exploit its divisions, playing off one group against another, particularly making use of Hedilla, who was unsophisticated and naive. Hedilla's leadership was challenged by the more traditional upper-class friends of José Antonio, Agustín Aznar and Sancho Dávila, and in April 1937 he was deposed. But he fought back, and both he and the Aznar and Dávila faction moved armed supporters into Salamanca while Franco sat back and watched events develop. Hedilla was led to believe, erroneously, that Franco would give him full control of the Falange after the defeat of the aristocratic faction. On 17 April 1937 fighting broke out in which two Falangists from different groups were killed. On 18 April the Falange National Council re-elected Hedilla as leader, but only by a minority of votes with several abstentions. Another meeting was planned for 19 April but at this point Franco stepped in and announced the merger of the Falange and the Carlists. On 19 April a Decree of Unification created a single party, the *Falange Española Tradicionalista y de las JONS* (usually known by its initials, the FET). The party symbol was the Falange yoke and arrows and its new uniform combined the Falange blue shirt and the Carlist red beret.

Superficially the Falange might appear to be in a predominant position in Nationalist politics, but Franco had in fact out-manoeuvred it and effectively taken it over. Serrano Súñer became the General Secretary of the FET and half the members of its Secretariat or executive were appointed by Franco. The imprecise description of the Falange as a 'movement' helped Franco to impose his own stamp upon it. Hedilla was merely offered a post as a member of its executive committee and, when he refused it, was arrested, imprisoned and not released till 1941. The Hedilla faction, and also some Carlists, were disgruntled at Franco's coup, but there was little they could do without being accused of disrupting the war effort. Franco had succeeded in ending the independence of the Spanish fascist move-

General Franco reviewing his troops

ment. José Antonio was incorporated into Falangist mythology with the cult of 'the absent one' but this was only window-dressing. 'Forced to accept Franco as their new leader, the Falangists saw their ideological role usurped by the church, their party turned into a machine for the distribution of patronage and their "revolution" indefinitely postponed.'[1]

As for the Alfonsist monarchists, their political organisation had largely melted away by the beginning of 1937. For a time Franco was careful not to disillusion them about the future of the monarchy since he needed them to offset the Falangists, but he had no intention of relinquishing power to Alfonso.

Finally, Franco's luck held again when his only remaining potential rival, Mola, was killed in an aircrash in northern Spain in June 1937. As Faupel, the German ambassador, commented, 'Franco undoubtedly feels relieved by the death of General Mola.'[2]

There were political crises in both the Nationalist and Republican zones in the Spring of 1937, but the outcomes were quite different. Not only were the Nationalists' problems less traumatic but they were more quickly and easily resolved with the subordination of the political parties to Franco's strong central leadership. As seen in Chapter 4, the Republic's crisis culminated in the fighting between the Communists, POUM and anarchists in Barcelona in May 1937. But although the Communists and their allies were the victors, this did not noticeably strengthen the government but instead left a legacy of bitterness and mistrust.

3 Franco's Regime

Franco was a tactician who concentrated on dealing with immediate problems, rather than a long-term political strategist. As Sheelagh Ellwood points out, 'rarely can anyone have been so successful at holding on to power while appearing to have nothing to do with politics'.[3] His political statements were often vague and meaningless, perhaps deliberately so, as for example his declaration in October 1936 that 'Spain would be organised within a wide-ranging totalitarian concept of unity and continuity'.[4] But in practice he aimed at an orderly and disciplined state, rather than a totalitarian one. In so far as it had an ideological basis, his regime was modelled on the military hierarchy he had always admired in the army. Franco can be defined as much by what he was opposed to as by what he stood for. He abhorred liberalism, democracy, communism and socialism, and also freemasonry (which at that time was associated with liberalism), and was convinced that a combination of these had ruined Spain and caused her decline from great power status. He believed in strong authoritarian government and also in centralisation - regional autonomy was abolished and the Catalan and Basque languages prohibited. Franco was very much in agreement with the monarchist view of society, though he himself was to be the new monarch.

He found it expedient to develop his own personality cult with ceremony, ritual and propaganda. Posters and photographs of the *Caudillo* appeared everywhere and national holidays reinforced his importance, for example 1 October, the Day of Caudillo. 1936 was the 'first triumphal year' in the new Francoist calendar. The photograph on page 104 shows a victorious Franco reviewing Italian troops at the end of the war. Note Franco's pre-eminent position in the ceremony, the inscription above the coat of arms which refers to Spain 'one, great and free'.

But while his title reflected those of the *Duce* and *Führer*, Franco's regime sought to resurrect the values of sixteenth-century Spain rather than develop those of a twentieth-century fascist state. Franco's

A Nationalist poster

Spain has aptly been described as a 'recreation of reign of Catholic Kings with Italian fascist trimmings'.[5] The Civil War was regularly referred to as a Crusade and depicted as a new *Reconquista* (a reference to the expulsion of the Moors in Medieval times). The emphasis in propaganda was on tradition, a return to the pious and nationalist values of the fifteenth-century Catholic Kings, Ferdinand and Isabella. Falangist symbols co-existed with references to the conquistadors, the sixteenth century Spanish conquerors of Mexico and Peru. The propaganda poster on page 106, with its combination of sixteenth and twentieth-century figures, illustrates the continuity which was made between contemporary and traditional values, and the way in which the past was used to legitimise the present.

Franco's regime rested primarily on the Church, the army and the conservative groups. His first government, established in January 1938, contained all acceptable political views and included monarchists and generals, together with tame Falangists. Serrano Súñer was given a key post as Minister of the Interior. There were three generals, two Alfonsine monarchists and the Carlist, Rodezno. Falangists got only two posts as Ministers of Agriculture and Labour. This government set the tone for all later ones in being essentially a balancing act between all the Nationalist interest groups.

The Catholic Church was a main bulwark of Franco's regime. With one or two exceptions, the hierarchy were happy to follow the lead of the primate, Cardinal Gomá Archbishop of Toledo, in justifying and legitimising the rising. A few had misgivings about the savagery of the repression and the killings of civilians, but the Basque priests were an exception in supporting the Republic - many, in consequence were executed by the Nationalists. Pope Pius XI was initially reluctant to fully endorse the Nationalists, probably because of their links with the Nazi regime with which he was at odds, but in August 1937 the Vatican recognised the Nationalist government and sent an ambassador.

The support of the Church was not surprising since its privileges, including control of most of the education system, were restored. Religious instruction was re-introduced in all schools and anti-church books were banned. Most clergy had, in any case, been antagonised by the anti-clericalism of the Second Republic and the spate of church burnings and killings of priests which followed the rising. Soviet intervention on the side of the Republic further intensified their fears, and the war was frequently portrayed in propaganda as a Crusade to preserve Christian civilisation against atheistic communism.

Franco had subordinated the Falange but it did retain nominal control of much of the press - the Falange paper *Arriba* was one of the few permitted to be published in Nationalist Spain - and of the official youth movement. One area where it was allowed a significant say was that of labour relations. The Labour Charter issued in March 1938 reflected Falange ideas and contained several references to workers' rights such as the right to work, security of employment, minimum wages, holidays with pay and family allowances. Based on the Italian fascist model, 28 Syndicates representing different branches of industry were to be set up to replace the trade unions. These were supposed to include employers as well as workers but this did not happen in practice since Franco had no intention of antagonising businessmen or landowners. In theory the syndicates claimed to be establishing a fascist model of society which would transcend class and other social distinctions, but in reality this amounted to very little and few of the points in the Charter were put into action.

4 Daily Life in Nationalist Spain

a) The economy and standards of living

Though affected by the all-pervading military atmosphere, life in the Nationalist zone carried on more normally than in the Republic. For one thing there were no air-raids. Though there were calls for the public to donate gold and jewellery and economise by limiting themselves to a one course meal on one day of the week, standards of living did not greatly deteriorate. Prices were controlled, though they had risen more rapidly than wages by the end of the war. There was plenty of foreign credit and the Nationalists had a major advantage in having greater supplies of food, which increased as they gained more territory. When a Republican town was captured, lorry loads of white bread would be rushed in, to emphasise the contrast between the two zones. The economic situation improved even further when the industrial areas in the north were taken over in 1937. There were even a few new enterprises, such as drainage schemes and the establishment of a cotton industry in Andalusia.

On the negative side has to be set the abolition of trade unions and of collective bargaining, the bans on political activity except through the FET, and the continual terror experienced by those who disagreed with the regime. However, for those who backed Franco, especially in the upper and middle class, life went on much as before. This account of a typical day in the life of a Nationalist pilot in San Sebastian in 1938 portrays a carefree existence which would be very different from that of his counterpart in the Republic:

8.30 Breakfast with the family.
9.30 Take-off for the front; bombard enemy batteries; machine gun convoys and trenches.
11.00 Rudimentary golf in the club at Lasarte.
12.30 Sunbathing on the Ondarreta beach and quick splash in the calm sea.
13.30 Shellfish, beer and a chat in a café in the Avenue.

14.00 Lunch at home.
15.00 Short siesta.
16.00 Second sorty, similar to this morning's.
18.30 Cinema.
21.00 Aperitif in the Bar Basque. Good 'Scotch', animated atmosphere.
22.15 Dinner at the Nicolasa Restaurant, war songs, camaraderie. enthusiasm.[6]

b) The position of women

Attitudes to women also contrasted sharply with those in the Republic. The Nationalists held traditional views on gender roles and believed firmly in separate and unequal spheres, regarding women's place as in the home and family, rather than at work or in public life. Their attitudes to women and the family reflected those promoted in Germany and Italy by Hitler and Mussolini. Pilar Primo de Rivera, the sister of José Antonio, stated, 'What we shall never do is put women in competition with men because women will never succeed in equalling men; if they try, women will lose the elegance and grace necessary for a life together with men.'[7] Civil marriage and divorce laws were repealed, large families encouraged and girls were educated separately in such as way as to fit them for roles of wife and mother. There were campaigns against immodest dress and make-up.

The war did provide some women with a role outside the home, albeit supportive of men. The Falange and the Carlists both had women's sections, and volunteer organisations were established such as 'Women in the service of Spain' and 'Work aiding the front'. The most important was the Falange women's section, led by Pilar Primo de Rivera, which through the *Auxilio Social* provided soup kitchens, collected money for the destitute, and ran orphanages. From 1937 all women aged between 17 and 35, with no family responsibilities, had to undertake duties in the war effort and there were some women working in war industries. However, most of this involvement ceased when the war ended.

c) Terror and repression

It is estimated that at least 80,000 people were killed in the Nationalist zone during and just after the war. Many more were imprisoned or sent to forced labour camps. Nationalist terror was, from the first, an officially approved and deliberate policy designed to intimidate the population of captured territories. Nationalist repression was greater than in the Republic and as the Nationalists conquered additional territory they set out to subdue the potentially hostile inhabitants. Franco himself played a direct role, authorising many of the death sentences.

At the beginning of the war martial law was established and military courts set up. As the Army of Africa advanced northwards from Seville, Republican sympathisers were systematically killed in all the towns which were taken. The most well-publicised example was at Badajoz near the Portuguese frontier, where, in August 1936, about 2,000 people, including anyone who could be proved to have belonged to the Republican militias, were shot. The events in Badajoz are described in the following extract, an eyewitness account by an American journalist:

1 We drove straight to the Plaza. Here yesterday there was a ceremonial, symbolic shooting. Seven leading Republicans of the Popular Front shot with a band and everything before three thousand people. To prove that Rebel generals didn't shoot only workers and peasants ... Suddenly we
5 saw two Falangists halt a strapping fellow in a workman's blouse and hold him while a third pulled back his shirt, baring his right shoulder. The black and blue marks of a rifle butt could be seen ... The report was unfavourable. To the bull ring with him ...
   ... peasants in blue blouses, mechanics in jumpers. 'The Reds.' They
10 are still being rounded up. At four o'clock in the morning they are turned out into the ring through the gate ... There machine guns await them.[8]

The 500 people killed in Granada in the Summer of 1936 included the poet and playwright García Lorca. When the Nationalists captured Málaga in February 1937, 4,000 opponents were executed and refugees fleeing along the coast road were shelled from the sea and bombed and machine-gunned.

Repression continued for some years after the war, when large numbers of people who had supported the Republic continued to be shot or imprisoned. Several prominent Republicans who had taken refuge in France were returned to Spain by the Gestapo in 1940 and executed. In February 1939 a Retroactive Law on Political Responsibilities made punishable any subversion from October 1934 to the outbreak of the war. An atmosphere of fear prevailed, where any individual connected with the Republic might be denounced. At the best, erstwhile Republicans were reduced to being second-class citizens and denied jobs and incomes.

Along with physical repression went intellectual repression. Political debate was forbidden and suspect books were banned or ceremonially burned. Miguel de Unamuno, Spain's most distinguished philosopher, had been removed from his post at the University of Salamanca in 1936 for criticising the regime. Press censorship was introduced. A Press Law of April 1938 allowed only registered publications to appear and registered journalists to work.

5 Franco's Relations with his Allies, 1936 to 1945

During the Civil War Franco's relationships with the Germans and

Italians were necessarily outwardly amicable, though beneath the surface they were often strained. Most of the disputes were about military strategy and Franco had to endure much unwanted advice from Mussolini, who did not disguise his contempt for the Spaniards' military abilities. There was also the possibility that the dictators would try to intervene politically. Mussolini, in particular, had ambitions to influence Spanish ideology and to make Spain into a fascist client state. Fortunately for Franco, neither he nor Hitler did much in practice to promote the Falange and Franco was able to keep them at arm's length politically, so that they never acquired anything like the influence that the Soviet Union attained in the Republic.

Germany wanted economic gains rather than direct political influence, hoping to acquire supplies of Spanish ores and minerals such as iron ore, tungsten, copper and lead, which were important to the German armaments industry. At the start of the war two companies HISMA and ROWAK were set up, the first based in Spain and the second in Berlin, to manage all trade between Germany and the Nationalists. Franco tried to keep economic concessions to a minimum, declaring in Summer 1937 'I would prefer to lose everything before giving up or mortgaging a particle of our national wealth.'[9] But in July 1937, needing German aid to repel the Republican offensive at Brunete, he had to agree to grant Germany most favoured nation status and to trade in raw materials. In October 1937 he backtracked, announcing that all foreign titles to mines and mining rights were null and void, and stalled the Germans for some months. However, in November 1938 the Nationalists badly needed new supplies following the Ebro offensive and Germany finally got 75 per cent of the shares in mining companies under the so-called Montana Project.

Franco's close relations with Germany and Italy continued after the end of the Civil War. A German-Spanish agreement in March 1939 provided for consultation in the event of an international crisis and Spain joined the Anti-Comintern Pact in March 1939. During the Second World War, Franco was extremely pro-German. It used to be thought that he shrewdly kept Spain out of the war by the exercise of skill and cunning, but this view is now disputed. Instead, research has shown that Franco and his chief confidant, Serrano Súñer, were firmly convinced of Axis victory, especially after the fall of France in 1940, and were eager to join in the war, being deterred only by Hitler's lack of enthusiasm for Spanish participation and unwillingness to meet their terms. In any case avoidance of entry into the war was 'less a victory for prudence than a necessity given a prostrate economy, an ill-equipped army and the Allies' stranglehold over vital imports'.[10]

In June 1940 Spain adopted non-belligerent status, which was a move away from neutrality, and could be seen as a step towards entry into the war. Franco wanted territory in the Mediterranean and North

Africa, especially Gibraltar and French Morocco. Possession of Gibraltar would have been a considerable gain for Hitler, but in other respects he felt Spanish participation in the war would not be advantageous given Spain's poor military and economic state. As well as territory Franco was demanding supplies of grain and fuel and the financing of the Spanish armed forces. In the Summer of 1940 Hitler had little interest in Spanish participation on these terms, while Spain's demands for territory had to be balanced by Hitler's need to conciliate both Italy and the French Vichy government.

Therefore, when Súñer visited Berlin in September 1940 he found the Germans less enthusiastic than expected, and the Spanish requests were countered by a German demand for bases in the Canaries and economic claims in mainland Spain and Morocco. The key meeting was held at Hendaye railway station on the French frontier on 23 October 1940, between Franco, Hitler, Súñer and Ribbentrop, the German Foreign Minister. Franco was still anxious to enter the war at a suitable moment in order to reap the rewards. But the Spanish demands for French Morocco were not met by Hitler, though a Protocol was signed which committed Spain to go to war at a future date to be decided. Hitler clearly thought Spanish entry into the war would cost more than it was worth.

In spite of the damp squib of Hendaye, Franco's loyalty to the Axis was largely undimmed, and throughout the war he allowed German U boats and planes to re-fuel on Spanish territory and provided facilities for aircraft reconnaissance and intelligence gathering and exported raw materials to Germany. And in June 1941 Spain adopted a position of 'moral belligerency' - a step nearer to joining in the war. In 1941 50,000 Falangist 'volunteers' went off to participate in the Russian campaign.

However, as the war went on, Franco was gradually moved away from the idea of active participation, encouraged by offers of economic help from the USA and Britain. As a British official put it in November 1940, 'the Spaniards are up for sale and it is our job to see that the auctioneer knocks them down to our bid'.[11] He never quite lost his faith in Axis victory but was more concerned with staying in power should the Allies win, and was careful in public to take an anti-Soviet, rather than a pro-Axis, line. By October 1943 he had moved back to 'vigilant neutrality'.

After the war Franco remained secretly pro-Axis. More than one hundred active Nazis and some Italian fascists were provided with asylum and new identities in Spain, and German property and assets in Spain were protected.[12]

6 Franco and Fascism

One of the most important questions to be asked about Nationalist Spain is whether, and to what extent, Franco and his regime can be

described as fascist. The Republicans always referred to their opponents as 'fascists' and it is still usual to bracket Franco with Hitler and
Mussolini as one of the trio of European fascist dictators. But some
studies of Franco and fascism have revised this view, and many historians, citing his lack of interest in fascist ideology and his subordination of the Falange, have come to see Franco as more an old-style military dictator than a fascist one. Carsten, for example considers that
Franco 'was a conservative of the old school, and his revolt a putsch by
the army leaders, not a social and national revolution.'[13] Views of
Franco's regime are inevitably coloured by the fact that, unlike his
fellow dictators, he survived and his regime in some respects became
less 'fascist' with the passage of time.

The issue is complicated by the problem of defining fascism. The
term has sometimes been loosely used to describe any twentieth
century right-wing dictatorship, but this is too broad a definition.
Many historians now doubt whether there is a satisfactory description
of fascism which fits even the inter-war dictatorships. For example,
Nazism in Germany had specific and unique characteristics, not least
the centrality of its racial ideology, in which it differed from fascism in
Italy. Nationalist Spain was much more susceptible to Italian influ-
ences than to German, and though there are also differences between
the Spanish and Italian states, it is with Italian fascism that Franco's
regime should be compared.

A lot also depends on the parameters of the debate - should it focus
only on the Falange to the exclusion of other groups? Attention has
usually been concentrated on the power and position of the Falange
and its relations with Franco. But Paul Preston argues that the study of
fascism in Spain should be broadened to take into account the role
and views of the army and other right-wing groups such as the CEDA
and the monarchists.[14] He stresses the similarities in aim between
these groups and the Falange during the Second Republic and the
rising. Though they were not ostensibly fascist, he considers that they
were in reality promoting a fascist society, not least by their support of
the interests of large property owners and their brutal repression of
the left. Martin Blinkhorn also argues that the Spanish right before
and after 1936 was 'objectively fascist', which means that in vigorously
supporting upper-class interests and in suppressing the left, and in its
commitment 'to some sort of authoritarian corporate state,' it played
a role analogous to that which fascism played in Italy.[15]

The main problem with this argument, however, is that as well as
discounting the fact that the Falange in Spain came to have less power
than the Fascist Party in Italy, it disregards Franco's political views,
seeing him as little more than an unwitting tool of Spanish capitalist
interests. But Franco had his own agenda and, to a great extent,
imposed his own wishes. His precise views are sometimes difficult to
identify since what he said varied according to circumstances. It is
impossible to say how far his eulogies of Hitler and Mussolini, and his

adoption of some of the forms of fascism, were designed to conciliate his fellow dictators or placate the Falange, and how far they stemmed from his own personal preferences. But against the view that he was a genuine fascist are his early political ideas and his relations with, and treatment of, the Falange. Unlike Mussolini in Italy, Franco did not get to power as the leader of a fascist party. Also, he made little real attempt to implement a social revolution on fascist lines, being content to leave the Spanish economic and social structure largely intact.

A point in favour of those who believe there was an affinity between Franco and fascism is his enthusiastic support for Germany during the Second World War even when the latter was losing. But was this the result of ideological commitment? Franco had every reason to be grateful to the Axis powers and would naturally lean towards them rather than the Allies, but he also very much wanted to be on the winning side, hoped to make territorial gains and found it hard to adjust to changing circumstances in the latter stages of the war. A key issue here is the extent to which the regime should be identified with Franco himself.

One method of simplifying and quantifying this question is to compile a list of the main similarities and differences between Franco's regime and that of Mussolini.

Similarities

1. Like those of Hitler and Mussolini, Franco's regime was a one-party dictatorship. The cult of the Caudillo paralleled those of the Führer and the Duce.

2. Franco's regime was anti-communist, anti-socialist, anti-parliamentarian and anti-democratic. Like Hitler and Mussolini, he banned trade unions and persecuted the left.

3. Like his fellow dictators, Franco was strongly nationalist, wishing to restore Spanish greatness, for example by acquiring colonies in North Africa. His aim to re-invent past glories can be compared with Mussolini's desire to re-create the Roman Empire.

4. The Labour Charter imitated Italian fascist policies. Attitudes to women and the family were similar to those prevailing in Germany and Italy.

5. Franco's post civil war economic policies, which emphasised autarky or self-sufficiency, were similar to those adopted in Germany and Italy.

6. Neither Franco nor Mussolini adopted racial views, apart from some limited lip-service to anti-Semitism.

Differences

1. Franco came to power through an army coup, not through the support of a fascist party. The army was always far more

---

dominant in Franco's Spain than was the Falange.

2. Franco had no connection with the Falange or with fascism prior to the rising.

3. Franco subdued the Falange and balanced it against other interest groups.

4. Franco was primarily an army commander and the army played a much greater political role in Nationalist Spain than in either Germany or Italy.

5. The Church had a prominent role in Franco's Spain (though Mussolini also had to conciliate the Papacy).

6. Franco's regime drew much of its inspiration from the past, rather than looking to establish a new social system.

7. Less was done than in Italy, to change economic or social life. Franco wanted to revert to the social class system which had prevailed before the Second Republic; he had no wish to implement a social revolution.

Having weighed up the similarities and differences you can see that the debate on whether Franco's Spain was a military dictatorship in the traditions of the nineteenth century Spanish right or a fascist state, is still open.

References

1 Paul Preston, *A concise history of the Spanish Civil War* (Fontana Press, 1996), pp.153-54.
2 Ibid, p.155.
3 Sheelagh Ellwood, *Franco* (Longman, 1994), p.223.
4 Ibid, p.90.
5 Raymond Carr, *The Spanish Tragedy* (Weidenfeld & Nicolson, 1977), p.209.
6 Quoted in Preston, *A concise history of the Spanish Civil War*, pp.164-65.
7 Ronald Fraser, *Blood of Spain* (Penguin, 1981), p.309.
8 Quoted in V. Cunningham (ed), *Spanish Front, writers on the Civil War* (OUP, 1986), pp.105-6.
9 Preston, *Franco*, p.286.
10 Raymond Carr, *Spain 1808-1975* (Clarendon Press, 1982), p.714.
11 Paul Preston, *The politics of revenge, fascism and the military in 20th century Spain* (Routledge, 1995), p.62.
12 Paul Preston, 'Franco's Nazi haven' in *History Today,* July 1997, pp.8-10.
13 F.L. Carsten, *The rise of Fascism* (Batsford, 1982), p.201.
14 Paul Preston, *The politics of revenge, fascism and the military in 20th century Spain* (Routledge, 1995), p.8.
15 Martin Blinkhorn, *Democracy and Civil War in Spain 1931-1939* (Routledge, 1988), p.57.

Summary Diagrams

Nationalist Spain, July 1936 to March 1939 and beyond

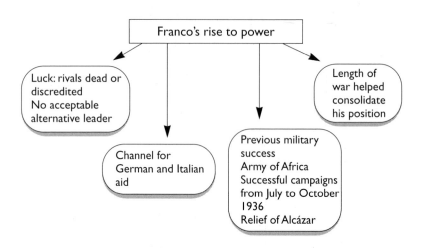

Franco's rise to power

- Luck: rivals dead or discredited
No acceptable alternative leader
- Channel for German and Italian aid
- Previous military success
Army of Africa
Successful campaigns from July to October 1936
Relief of Alcázar
- Length of war helped consolidate his position

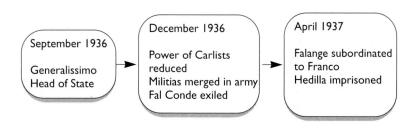

September 1936

Generalissimo
Head of State

→ December 1936

Power of Carlists reduced
Militias merged in army
Fal Conde exiled

→ April 1937

Falange subordinated to Franco
Hedilla imprisoned

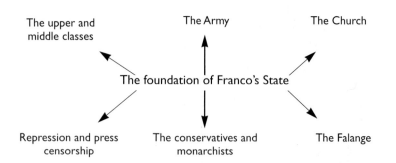

The upper and middle classes

The Army

The Church

The foundation of Franco's State

Repression and press censorship

The conservatives and monarchists

The Falange

Franco and his Allies

During the Civil War	During the Second World War
Discouraged interference in political and military affairs Little Italian influence but German economic gains	Franco eager to join the war but German refusal to meet his demands for economic aid and territory Key meeting at Hendaye in October 1940 Less enthusiastic from 1943 onwards when Germany losing

Essay questions on 'Nationalist Spain, July 1936 to March 1939'

These questions tend to fall into two types: those dealing with how Franco obtained or kept power, and those which require a comparison of his regime with those of Mussolini and Hitler. These are some examples:

1. How was Franco able to achieve power so easily and to retain it throughout the Civil War?
2. Assess the qualities of General Franco as a military leader and as ruler of Spain in the period 1936 to 1939.
3. How was Nationalist Spain during the Civil War able to acquire a much greater degree of unity than the Republic?
4. In what ways did the aims and ideas of Franco's supporters resemble, and differ from, those of the supporters of Mussolini and of Hitler?
5. To what extent can Franco's regime be described as fascist?

8 Conclusion: Spain since 1939

Franco continued to govern Spain until his death in November 1975. During his long rule, although he was occasionally challenged, his position was never seriously threatened.

It is tempting to see the Franco years as a static period in Spanish history. This impression is misleading, since they witnessed a number of important changes. Franco's aim was to incorporate all the different factions and 'political families' in the *Movement*, as the Francoist groups were termed, but the power balance between these groups altered over time in response to developments within Spain or from outside. For example, the Falange was more important during the war than later. It continued to control the state trade unions, the press, propaganda, the youth organisation and was entrenched in government bureaucracies; *Cara al sol* ('Face to the sun') the Falange anthem, was played regularly on public occasions and on Spanish radio until the 1960s. But this concealed the fact that its influence declined after 1945, relative to that of other groups.

Spanish history from 1939 to 1975 can be divided into two main periods. The first, from 1939 to the late 1950s, was a period when power was shared between the Falange, the monarchists and the army. The second, from the early 1960s to Franco's death, brought to prominence the so-called 'technocrats' distinguished more by their expertise as economists or administrators than by their political views. From 1969 the political basis of the regime was inexorably undermined as Franco's hold weakened due to his advancing age and ill-health.

1 Spain from 1939 to 1957

During the Second World War the Falange competed for influence with the army and the monarchists. Falangists were naturally enthusiastically pro-Axis, while their rivals were more neutral or tended to favour the Allies, especially when they could see that the latter were winning. These rivalries became so acute that they erupted in fighting between Falangists and Carlists in Bilbao in August 1942. Franco settled the matter by dismissing both Varela, the Carlist Minister for War, and Serrano Súñer, the leading pro-Falangist. In the end, as seen in the previous chapter, Spain kept out of the war, because, fortunately as it turned out for Franco, Hitler would not pay his price.

Franco's problems in balancing the political groups were made more difficult by the fact that those Nationalists who favoured the restoration of the monarchy were emboldened by the Allied success in the War. In September 1943 several generals petitioned Franco for the return of Don Juan, the son of Alfonso XIII (who had died in 1941). Franco ignored them, as he later ignored Don Juan's

'Lausanne address' of March 1945 which called on him to abandon power. The months just prior to and after Germany's defeat were a dangerous time for Franco given his extremely pro-Axis stand. He survived partly because the Allies had no intention of directly intervening in Spain and left the initiative up to Spaniards. Franco's opponents within Spain were also reluctant to act since they feared that any attempt to remove him might lead to renewed civil war. His enemies outside Spain were politically divided between Republicans, Socialists and monarchists. The exiled Socialist opposition to Franco got nowhere. They mounted some guerrilla activities in Spain but these failed and were abandoned by 1948. In the event Don Juan came to terms with Franco in 1948, allowing his son Juan Carlos to be

Memorial cross in the 'valley of the fallen'

educated in Spain. Franco's position was reinforced by the Law of Succession of March 1947 which announced that Spain was a kingdom but that Franco was Head of State for life with the right to nominate his successor. This was agreed by the Cortes, which had been reconvened in 1943, though with no power, and endorsed in a referendum.

But though Franco survived, Spain at the end of the Second World War was 'isolated and alone, ostracised by the victors,'[1] and refused admittance to the United Nations, though this snub had the effect of rallying support for Franco within Spain. Diplomatic isolation was only ended by the onset of the Cold War which rehabilitated Spain as the 'sentry of the west' against communism, and made her an ally of the United States. The Cold War made Franco's anti-communism an asset instead of a liability and an agreement with the USA in 1953 provided for American bases in Spain and also for much needed American loans. Spain was finally allowed into the UN in 1955.

Spain also faced severe economic problems which were not wholly the result of war but owed much to Franco's misguided economic policies which, like those of Hitler and Mussolini, emphasised self-sufficiency and aimed to reduce dependence on imports. These policies cut Spain off from much needed imports of food and from the foreign investment required to revive industry. Franco was committed to restoring the social structures which had existed before the Second Republic. Landowners and to a lesser extent small peasants (who got security of tenure at fixed rents), benefited, but agricultural labourers and urban wage-earners were worse off than ever. Real wages in 1951 were only 60 per cent of their 1936 level.

The extract below is an account by a visitor to Spain in 1949. Note that even though the general picture is one of deprivation, there are also indications of the beginning of a building boom and a tourist industry.

1   In a Madrid hotel the valet de chambre had been caught by the Civil War in Madrid where his sympathies had lain with the Nationalists. Yet the picture he painted of present conditions was sombre in the extreme. The black market, he declared, was the only business in the country that was
5   flourishing. Everyone from the highest authority down was in it ...

    'Spain', he went on, 'is finished. Everyone who can leave is doing so. If the frontiers were opened tomorrow half the population would walk out. If you could find me a job in London I would be deeply grateful.'

    Like everyone else he complained of the cost of living ... There has
10 been a severe inflation and everyone except the landowners and nouveaux riches are finding it hard to make ends meet ...

    How do the working class who cannot afford to live on the black market manage to keep alive? One way is by having extra ration books. New births are registered that have not occurred, deaths are concealed
15 and so forth. There is even a trade in ration books.

One of the things that most astonishes me in Madrid is the amount of building that has been done since the Civil War. Everywhere one sees new blocks of flats, business premises, ministries, mostly of a very large size ...

20 [In southern Spain] we went out to look at the new villas that were springing up. Marbella, thirty miles to the west, has been turned into a fashionable plage [beach] and now this is happening in Torremolinos too. [2]

Meanwhile, Franco was determined to keep the Civil War and its lessons alive. Those who had been on the wrong side faced continued repression, and many opponents of Franco were still in prison or in labour camps in the 1950s and after. The themes of the war, especially its presentation as a crusade against communism, were perpetuated in propaganda, which emphasised the division into victors and vanquished. The grandiose war memorials which were built by forced labour in the 'valley of the fallen' near Madrid, commemorated only the Nationalists' losses. (See the photograph on page 119 of this massive memorial crowned by a huge cross.)

After 1945 Franco tried to dissociate himself from the Axis, though this complete change of viewpoint was not very convincing given his war-time views. The Falange enjoyed less influence, and more power passed to Catholic, ex-CEDA politicians, many associated with the Catholic Action pressure group. Accidentalist, like the CEDA during the Second Republic (see Chapter 2), and pragmatic, these men were prepared to forget a monarchical restoration for the time being and to make the best of Franco. The period from 1951 to 1957 also saw cautious moves towards economic liberalism; autarky and state interventionism began to be abandoned in favour of a free market. Greater prosperity was to give the regime a new lease of life. Another boost was a Concordat (agreement) with the Vatican in 1953. Meantime Spain began to divest itself of its remaining colonies and Morocco was granted independence in 1956. This seems a surprising move given Franco's attachment to the empire, but was made inevitable by the decline of the French empire in North Africa and the rise of Arab nationalism.

2 Spain from 1957 to 1975

From the late 1950s Franco took more of a back seat, playing a less prominent role in the day to day running of the government, devoting himself instead to leisure pursuits such as hunting and fishing. He delegated most of his Head of Government responsibilities to the vice-president of the Cabinet, appointing Agustín Grandes to this post in 1962 and Carrero Blanco in 1967. From 1957 more university trained 'technocrats' began to enter government and the civil service. These were people with economic or managerial expertise, many with connections with the Catholic organisation 'Opus Dei' (Work of God), which was on the 'liberal' wing of the Church.

Economic changes were more apparent than political ones. Economic improvements were a necessity if inflation and balance of payments deficits were to be overcome, foreign investment attracted and conditions of entry to the European Economic Community satisfied. The abandonment of economic isolation, together with more integration into the European economy, resulted in the 'economic miracle' of the 1960s, with the establishment of manufacturing and tourist industries. There was a small increase in real wages especially in industry, though expenditure on education or social services remained low. More white collar jobs in the service sector were available, including more jobs for women. The urban population grew as more rural workers migrated to the towns. Many Spaniards also sought work in other parts of Europe.

But economic improvements were not matched by political reform and it was the absence of this which prevented Spain being admitted to the European Community (now the European Union) in 1962. And though most Spaniards seemed content with relative prosperity, social unrest increased. There were more strikes, with more employers prepared to negotiate with independent or illegal unions rather than with the official Falangist syndicates. As in other parts of Europe, a radical student movement developed in the 1960s. There was a revival of Catalan and particularly of Basque nationalism, the latter involving terrorist activities, assassinations and bank robberies. The Basque terrorist organisation (ETA) assassinated Carrero Blanco (Franco's deputy) in 1973.

A few concessions were made, including more press freedom, but these did not satisfy the opposition, which, by the time of Franco's death, extended from Christian Democrats to Communists. From 1971, following a more liberal lead from the Vatican, the Spanish bishops and clergy gradually began to dissociate themselves from the regime. The army meantime was declining in importance. It had little to do apart from maintaining internal order, and by the 1960s was far too large for the diminishing tasks left to it.

Franco hated change and would have liked to resist it, but he had already named Prince Juan Carlos as his successor in 1969. When he died in November 1975, Falangists who hoped that the essential elements of Francoism would continue under the restored monarchy were to be quickly disabused.

3 Spain after Franco

After the accession of Juan Carlos events moved rapidly. The new king made it clear that he was not bound by the past and, with his Prime Minister Suarez, speedily engineered a return to democracy. Only a few people wished to preserve Francoism. The Franco years had mostly been characterised more by apathy than by active support for his regime. A new generation of Spaniards had grown up who remembered nothing of the Civil War and viewed it as a distasteful, even shameful, episode. Francoism was seen as not only illiberal but out of date, a view reinforced by the collapse of the Portuguese dictatorship in 1974. In 1977, therefore, democracy was restored, the Communist Party legalised, regional autonomy granted, and the first free elections held since 1936. They produced a decisive rejection of Francoisms with the great majority of the electorate voting for centre-left or centre-right parties. The changes were ratified in a new constitution, approved in a referendum in 1978. These reforms, unlike those of the Second Republic, met with general approval.

This transformation did not occur without resistance from the 'bunker', as the extreme right of die-hard Francoists were known. Falangist groups had already been active before Franco's death in attacking the left and promoting street fighting. The Falange and sections of the army, old rivals, but both now rendered anachronistic, combined in an attempt to put the clock back. In February 1981 a last army coup was attempted when Colonel Tejero invaded the Cortes with 200 civil guards. His aim was to take the members of the Cortes hostage, restore military government and overthrow democracy. Tejero's action was probably the tip of the iceberg of a deeper seated military plot which never got off the ground. In the event this last *pronunciamiento* was a total failure. The King acted decisively and made a TV broadcast condemning the attempted coup and thousands of Spaniards demonstrated against it. Within a few hours, in noticeable contrast with July 1936, it had collapsed.

The wheel had therefore come full circle and by the 1980s Spain was again a constitutional monarchy, this time with a Socialist government. But with the difference that this democracy was to be much more firmly based than that of the Second Republic.

References

1   Raymond Carr, *Spain 1808-1975* (Clarendon Press, 1982), p.714.
2   Gerald Brenan, *The face of Spain* (Turnstile Press, 1950), pp.25-29, 101-11.

Summary Diagram
Conclusion: Spain since 1939

Franco pro-Axis
Spain narrowly avoids joining
the War on the German side

Falange important but obliged
to share power with army
and monarchists

1939-1945

Economic problems:
food shortages, inflation,
low wages, autarky

Political problems:
Possible restoration of the
monarchy at the end of the war

Franco survives and
successfully balances
political groups

Diplomatic isolation to mid
1950s but becomes US ally in
the Cold War

1945-1957

Economic problems continue

Decline of the Falange relative
to other political groups

Franco takes a less prominent
role and support for
Francoism declines

More power for a-political
technocrats

1957-1975

Economic miracle:
boom in industry and tourism.
Some increase in wages

More unrest, strikes, Basque
nationalism

November 1975: death of Franco

Restoration of the monarchy under Juan Carlos

Democracy restored, free elections 1977

Falange/Army coup fails in February 1981

Chronological Table

1921	Spanish defeat in Morocco
1923 – 1930	Dictatorship of Primo de Rivera
1930 August	Republicans agree the Pact of San Sebastian
1931 12 April	Municipal elections
14 April	Alfonso XIII leaves Spain and Republic proclaimed
April **1931** – Nov **1933**	Left Republican governments in power, Church, Army and land reforms
1932 August	Sanjurjo rising
Nov **1933** – Feb **1936**	Right Republican governments in power, reforms reversed
1934 February	Fusion of Falange and JONS to form a fascist party under José Antonio
October	Asturias rising
1936 February	Popular Front government elected
July	Assassination of the monarchist leader, Calvo Sotelo
17-20 July	Rising in Morocco and major Spanish cities
July	Britain and France opt for a policy of non-intervention
July – August	Start of Revolution in Republican zone
August	Airlift of Army of Africa to mainland Spain
September	Largo Caballero becomes Prime Minister
September	First meeting of the Non-intervention Committee
September	Extremadura, San Sebastian, Toledo, fall to Nationalists
1 October	Franco takes office as head of Nationalist state
October	Soviet aid sent to the Republic
November	Battle for Madrid, Nationalists fail to take the city
1937 February	Battle of Jarama
March	Battle of Guadalajara
April	Beginning of Nationalist campaign in northern Spain
19 April	Franco unites the Falange and Carlists under his own leadership
26 April	Bombing of Guernica
3 May	Fighting between the rival Republican political groups in Barcelona
16 May	Largo Caballero resigns, Negrín becomes Prime Minister
June	Nationalists capture Bilbao
July	Failed Republican offensive at Brunete

August	Failed Republican offensive at Belchite
October	Nationalist conquest of the north complete
December	Republican offensive captures Teruel
1938 January	Franco's first Government
February	Nationalists recapture Teruel
April	Prieto resigns from Negrín's Government
April	Nationalists reach the Mediterranean, cutting Republic zone in two.
July	Beginning of Republican offensive on the Ebro
September	the Munich Conference
November	defeat of Ebro offensive
1939 January	Nationalists occupy Catalonia
March	Casado coup in Madrid
March	Nationalists occupy Madrid
1 April	Civil War ends

Glossary

Africanistas	Army officers with long service in Morocco
Bienio negro	The 'two black years' - a term used by left Republicans to describe reversal of reforms and repression under the Right Republic from 1933 to 1936
Carlists	Traditional monarchist/Catholic party based in Navarre, who supported the claim to the throne of Don Carlos, a descendant of a nineteenth-century pretender.
Caudillo	Military leader, the title given to Franco as Head of State
CEDA	*Confederación Española de Derechas Autónomas* - the federation of right-wing parties set up by Gil Robles in 1933
Civil Guards	Armed police force established in the nine-teenth century to keep internal order
CNT	*Confederación Nacional del Trabajo* - the Anarchist trade union
Comintern	Communist International - an organisation of Communist parties set up by the Soviet Union in 1919
Cortes	The Spanish parliament
Esquerra	The left-wing Catalan political party
FAI	*Federación Anarquista Ibérica* - the extreme revolu-tionary branch of the Anarchist movment
Falange	The Spanish fascist party established by José Antonio in 1933
FET	*Falange Española Tradicionalista* - the party estab-lished by Franco's decree in April 1937
Generalitat	Autonomous Catalan government
Latifundia	Large estates in southern Spain, mainly cultivated by landless labourers
Lliga	The conservative Catalan political party
Militias	Para-military groups of the various political parties
PCE	*Partido Communista de España* - the Spanish Communist Party founded in 1920
POUM	*Partido Obrero de Unificación Marxista* - an anti-Soviet Marxist party formed in 1935
Pronunciamiento	A military coup
PSUC	Partido Socialista Unificado de Cataluña - the Catalan combined Communist/Socialist party formed in 1936
PSOE	*Partido Socialista Obrero Español* - the Spanish Socialist Party founded in 1879

Requetés	The para-military organisation of the Carlists
SIM	*Servicio de Investigación Militar* - the Communist/Soviet secret police set up in 1937
UGT	*Unión General de Trabajadores* - the Socialist trade union

Further Reading

There are several useful general histories of the war. The starting point is undoubtedly Hugh Thomas's monumental work, *The Spanish Civil War* (Penguin, 1986 edition). This is a chronological history with a wealth of detail on the origins and events of the war, though it is sometimes difficult to disentangle the analytical points from the narrative. Paul Preston and Raymond Carr are two of the main authorities on Spain. Highly readable is Paul Preston, *A concise history of the Spanish Civil War* (Fontana Press, 1996). Also recommended is Raymond Carr, *The Spanish Tragedy* (Weidenfeld & Nicolson, 1977). Raymond Carr's, *Spain 1808-1975* (Clarenden, 1982), covers a wider time-span and is particularly useful in placing the war in context and on developments before and after the 1930s.

Sheelagh Ellwood, *The Spanish Civil War* (Basil Blackwell 1991), is an excellent summary of the war, while George Esenwein and Adrian Shubert's, *Spain at War* (Longman, 1995), is a recent work which approaches the subject in a thematic way. Chapter 7 is particularly good on the collectives. Martin Blinkhorn, *Democracy and Civil War in Spain 1931-1939* (Routledge, 1988), provides a first-rate introduction to the issues and controversies. Other general histories are Gabriel Jackson, *Concise history of the Spanish Civil War* (Thames and Hudson, 1974), and David Mitchell, *The Spanish Civil War* (New York, 1983).

Books with source material include Harry Browne, *Spain's Civil War* (Longman, second edition 1996), which is in the Seminar Studies series. Patricia Knight, *The Spanish Civil War* (Macmillan, 1991), is a collection of sources in the Documents and Debates series. Ronald Fraser, *Blood of Spain* (Penguin, 1981), is a unique oral history based on interviews with eyewitnesses and participants on both sides in the war. It contains some fascinating material but its format is slightly confusing with the section on the Republic placed at the end.

Among more detailed studies of particular aspects of the war are Raymond Carr (ed), *The Republic and Civil War* (Weidenfeld & Nicolson, 1977), and Paul Preston (ed), *Revolution and War in Spain* (Methuen, 1984).

The most recent, as well as the most comprehensive, biography of Franco is Paul Preston, *Franco* (Fontana Press, 1995), which has a very detailed section on the post 1939 period. Sheelagh Ellwood, *Franco* (Longman, 1994), is a shorter, more accessible account.

On Spanish fascism, pages 194 to 204 of F.L. Carsten, *The rise of Fascism* (Batsford, 1982), recount the history of the Falange and conclude that Nationalist Spain was more a traditional military dictatorship than a fascist state. On the other side of the argument, the first chapter of Paul Preston, *The politics of revenge, fascism and the military in 20th century Spain* (Routledge, 1990), presents a stimulating case for the view that Nationalist Spain was indeed fascist.

Numerous first-hand accounts of the war have been written by

Britons who participated on the Republic side and many of these are still in print. A good introduction to this genre is Valentine Cunningham (ed), *Spanish front, writers on the Civil War* (Oxford University Press, 1986), which contains a lively selection of writings by journalists and members of the International Brigades. George Orwell, *Homage to Catalonia* (Martin, Secker & Warburg, 1970), is the best contemporary account of the war, excellent for its descriptions of revolution, militias and the conflict between Communists and the POUM.

Lastly, don't on any account miss reading the two series of articles in *History Today*, July 1986 and March 1989, dealing with the Popular Front, the origins of the War, the military events, why the Republic lost and the aftermath of the war. Taken together these provide an excellent coverage of the main issues. Also try to see the Film 'Land and freedom' directed by Ken Loach and released in 1995. This graphically portrays issues of revolution, collectivisation, and the disputes between the Communists and their more left-wing rivals, seen through the eyes of a British volunteer.

Index

Many of the main topics can be located from the contents page

A selection of best-selling and related titles from Hodder & Stoughton *Educational*

Title	Author	ISBN	Price (UK)
War and Peace: International Relations 1914-45	David Williamson	0 340 57165 9	£6.50
France 1914-69: The Three Republics	Peter Neville	0 340 56561 6	£6.50
Germany, 1933-45: The Third Reich	Geoff Layton	0 340 53847 3	£6.50
Italy, Liberalism and Fascism, 1870-1945	Mark Robson	0 340 54548 8	£6.50

All Hodder & Stoughton *Educational* books are available from your local book shop, or can be ordered direct from the publisher. Just tick the titles you would like and complete the details below. Prices and availablilty are subject to change without prior notice.

Please enclose a cheque or postal order made payable to *Bookpoint Limited,* and send to: Hodder & Stoughton *Educational*, 39 Milton Park, Abingdon, Oxon OX14 4TD, UK. EMail address: orders @bookpoint.co.uk

UK postage will be charged at £2.00 for each book plus £2.30 for packing. Four books and above will be charged at 5% of the invoice value (minimum charge £5.00).

If you would like to pay by credit card, our centre team would be delighted to take your order by telephone. Our direct line (44) 01235 400414 (lines open 9.00am - 6.00pm, Monday to Saturday, with a 24 hour answering service). Alternatively you could send a fax to (44) 01235 400454.

Title _____ First name _____ Surname _____

Address _____

_____

_____

Postcode _____ Daytime telephone no. _____

If you would prefer to pay by credit card, please complete:

Please debit my Master Card / Access / Diner's Card / American Express (delete as applicable)

Card number _____

Expiry date _____ Signature _____

If you would like to receive further information on our products, please tick the box ☐